A

HAND-BOOK

OF

BENARES

A

HAND-BOOK

OF

BENARES

ARTHUR PARKER

GYAN

Published by

Gyan Publishing House
5, Ansari Road
Daryaganj, New Delhi-110002
Phone: 011-47034999, 9811692060
E-mail: books@gyanbooks.com

Distribution Network
gyanbooks.com
India, USA, Canada, UK, Australia

ISBN: 978-93-7014-459-0 (PB)

First Published, 1901

2nd Impression 2025

Printed at: Gyan Press, Delhi.

A HAND-BOOK OF BENARES
Author: ARTHUR PARKER

A HAND-BOOK OF BENARES,

BY THE

REV. ARTHUR PARKER,
LONDON MISSIONARY SOCIETY.

WITH A MAP OF THE CITY.

Second and Revised Edition.

Trivandrum:
PRINTED AT THE TRAVANCORE GOVERNMENT PRESS.

1901.

A

HAND-BOOK

OF

BENARES,

BY THE

REV. ARTHUR PARKER,

LONDON MISSIONARY SOCIETY.

WITH A MAP OF THE CITY.

Second and Revised Edition.

Trivandrum;

PRINTED AT THE TRAVANCORE GOVERNMENT PRESS,

1901.

PREFACE.

In this second edition of the 'Handbook to Benares' there are several important alterations. The Historical sketch has been to a great extent re-written and a number of corrections made here and there in other parts of the book, while the itineraries have been revised and, it is hoped, improved.

It is grievous to a lover of the grey old city to hear of so many visitors whose anticipations have been greater far than their realization. These are not usually people of an artistic temperament, for to such Benares, with its wonderful river front, is a mine of wealth. But to those who come from Agra, Delhi and Lucknow with their gorgeous and massive specimens of Muhammadan architecture, expecting to find here similar evidences of Hindu art, a great disappointment is inevitable. In truth the distinguishing feature of Benares is neither architectural magnificence nor artistic beauty in any form, and what it possesses of either of these is purely accidental, but as the home and shrine of the religious faith which sways the Hindu nations it is unique and unrivalled. Wonderful and fascinating, nay even awe-inspiring, Benares truly is, but she does not yield her secret easily. A guide-book can do little more than point out the beaten tracks and indicate where the treasures lie hid. Happy is the traveller who brings with him the wise and discerning eye and the sympathetic mind. Happier still if, in addition, he have the aid of a living guide—be he Indian or European—who will gently draw aside the veil which hides from the vulgar and hasty the secrets of the city's past glory and present power. Should the visitor be fortunate enough to meet such an one then this little book must be content to drop into a secondary place, and serve in after days to recall the out-line and retain the main features of a city of wonders.

ARTHUR PARKER.

Trivandrum, Travancore,
March, 1901.

CONTENTS.

		Page.
Preface.		
Chapter I.	Introduction	1
Chapter II.	A Historical Sketch	6
Chapter III.	Present-day Benares	23
Chapter IV.	Alphabetical list of Places and Object of Interest ...	29
Chapter V.	Hints to Travellers	79
	Index	83
	Rates of Hire of Hackney Carriages ...	85

MAP OF BENARES. To face Title page.

CHAPTER I.

Introduction.

The traveller who approaches Benares by railway from Calcutta may obtain from the carriage window one of the finest views of the city possible. As the train nears the great bridge which spans the broad bosom of the Ganges, the buildings on the northern side come slowly into view, and gradually grow on the sight till, stretched along the top of the lofty bank and looking down into the rippling waters, the city is seen sitting like a queen on her throne, with her spires and minarets standing clear out against the brilliant blue of the eastern sky, and the stone stairways of the ghats running out below into the sacred stream, surely one of the most imposing and impressive sights in all India.

The Dufferin Bridge which carries the Oude and Rohilkhand railway over the Ganges is a very fine structure, and a triumph of engineering skill. It is constructed of steel girders, rivetted together under hydraulic pressure, and rests on fifteen massive piers of masonry. The total length of the bridge is 3,568 feet, and it cost Rs. 1,727 per foot or over 75 lacs of rupees in all. Vehicles are allowed to pass over the bridge during the intervals of railway traffic and a path is provided on each side for foot passengers. It is strongly fortified at either end by massive towers, loop-holed and turretted and fitted with iron doors, so that a very small force would be able to defend it. It took over seven years in building, having been commenced in June 1880 and being formally opened by Lord Dufferin in October 1887.

Benares is the capital of a province which bears the same name and which includes the districts of Benares, Mirzapur, Jaunpur, Ghazipur and Ballia and contains a population of nearly five million souls. The city is the seat of the local Government and has a garrison made up of a wing of a British infantry regiment and a regiment of native infantry, all of whom are accommodated on the extensive plain which skirts the railway, north of the Cantonment Station.

The Cantonment, or European quarter, lies to the west of the city where the whitewashed bungalows of the foreign residents may be seen embowered in trees, and each set in its own compound.

There are two good hotels in the same quarter, Clarke's and the Hotel de Paris, the former being the oldest established. It is advisable to engage rooms before arrival, especially during the cool season from November to March.

The city, conservative though it is, has not been able to escape altogether the tide of change which has set in with British rule and the fine metalled roads which run from the Cantonment to the very heart of the city, are evidence of the presence of a practical and energetic race. The water-works which now supply the city with filtered water pumped up from the river, have conferred a boon much appreciated by the native population, though the smoke-stack of the pumping station, which rears its head among the spires at the southern end of the ghats, hardly adds to the beauty of the scene. The city is a great emporium of trade, especially in grain and native food stuffs generally. From the rich plains which surround the city vast quantities of wheat and rice, millet and lentils, as well as unrefined sugar pour into the bazaars for sale.

The manufactures of Benares have been famous for centuries not only in India, but throughout the world. Macaulay in his essay on Warren Hastings recalls the glories, now alas, in a great degree departed, of the city's fame in this respect. "Commerce," says he, "had as many pilgrims as religion. All along the shores of the venerable stream lay great fleets of vessels, laden with rich merchandise. From the looms of Benares went forth the most delicate silks that adorned the halls of St. James and of Versailles, and in the bazaars the muslins of Bengal and the sabres of Oude were mingled with the jewels of Golconda and the shawls of Cashmere."

The special productions for which Benares is now famous are embroidered cloth called kamkhwáb (kincob) work and engraved brass ware. The former is produced in considerable quantities and of a very fine quality, though it too often happens that the most sumptuous designs of gold and silver thread are worked upon very inferior velvet and satin. Very great manual skill is exhibited in the manufacture of the exceedingly fine gold and silver wire employed, and the designs are often very beautiful. Native workmen lament the gradual adoption of European dress by enlightened Indian noblemen and declare that on this account their trade has suffered very largely. Large quantities, however, must still be produced to decorate the beauties of the zanana, and also for use as ceremonial robes, and every great durbar or levee in India glitters with the rich brocaded silks and satins of Benares. Babu Debi Prasád, whose shop overlooks the Chauk is the best known dealer in these goods. Benares brass ware is a marketable commodity all over Europe. Most people are familiar—too familiar perhaps—with specimens of it, yet a walk through the Thatera Bazaar, as the brass workers' street is called, will well repay the visitor, for there he will see the ware being produced by the same primitive means as no doubt were employed centuries ago. The worker, often a mere child, sits cross-legged on the ground, and, using feet and toes as well as hands, by means of a tiny punch or chisel and a light hammer, unaided by tracings or models, works out on the surface of the metal the intricate and grotesque devices handed down through generations of workmen.

Wooden toys are also made in large quantities in the city. They are turned on very primitive lathes from a hard white wood and covered with lac varnish of the most brilliant colours, which are fortunately quite non-poisonous in character.

But the visitor will be chiefly interested in Benares as a religious centre. It has been fitly called "The sacred city of the Hindus," for no other can compare with it in the amount of religious merit it can confer on the devotee that enters its gates. Benares may well be considered to represent the very heart of Hinduism. Along the many roads that converge on the city, by the river, and by the railway, she draws to herself from all over the vast continent, continuous streams of devout and affectionate pilgrims. They come to her brimful of love and piety, and after a season spent in her temples and shrines and by her sacred stream, she sends them forth again, overflowing with zeal and enthusiasm, to carry her fame to the farthest borders of the land. There is not in all India a more fascinating or impressive sight than is presented on the ghats that line the river bank. There, day by day, thousands and thousands of devout Hindus, from all the tribes and nations of many peopled India, both men and women, meet to bathe in the sacred stream, and, under the direction of hundreds of Brahmin priests, to perform the thousand and one ceremonies of purification and prayer which their elaborate and exacting ritual prescribes. Any attempt to depict in words this wonderful scene must fall far short of the truth. Viewed from the river, the vast array of picturesque temples, monasteries and shrines, rich in carving and fretwork, which line the top of the bank stands out sharply defined against the blue sky, and forms a background to the animated scene beneath them. Up and down the immense stairways below passes an ever moving multitude of worshippers, arrayed in brilliantly coloured or dazzlingly white garments. Lower still, the eye falls on a dense mass of figures crowding the lowest steps of the ghats, some seated in meditation on the steps themselves, others lining the wooden piers thrust out into the water, but all, with intent gaze and muttering lips, engaged in ceaseless prayer. Among and around these again is a great multitude, breast high in the sacred stream, with a fixed ecstatic look engaged in washing away the impurities of soul and body alike. And from all goes up one continuous murmur of prayer and adoration, like the sound of a moaning wind over a distant forest. Eye and ear alike are filled and flooded with an indescribable and overwhelming multitude of sensations, and the heart is oppressed with the august meanings which lie behind this awe-inspiring sight. This is Benares! Here is laid bare the secret which for thousands of years, through vicissitudes the most terrible and changes the most radical, this wonderful city has held to itself and which now in these more peaceful times has given it a new lease of life! Here, if anywhere, is pourtrayed the very spirit of Brahmanism!

CHAPTER II.

A Historical Sketch.

Scarred by the brand of the blinding heat,
And the wrath divine, and the sins of man,
And the baleful tramp of the conqueror's feet,
It has suffered all since the world began.

The path of history is like the course of a river, which, broad and clear, with well-defined limits where it nears the abodes of men, when traced backwards winds and narrows, and finally hides its source in some dark forest or inaccessible mountain defile. This is emphatically the case with the history of Benares. The student has not far pursued the backward path before he finds himself baffled and perplexed by the scanty materials for knowledge, and very early—too early—the course of the history is lost in the tangled jungle of fable and legend wherein are hidden the origins of all things Indian.

By marking off the history into periods not too rigidly limited one may perhaps hope to compass the city's story. The first is the legendary or Pre-Buddhistic period whose hither limit is the rise of the religion of Gautama Buddha, some five and a half centuries before our era. Doubtless for long before that time there had been a city of shrines here, for to it, as to a centre of light and leading, journeyed the great teacher after his enlightenment "to set in motion the wheel of the excellent law." The so-called records of that fabled time fill many pages of the later Sanscrit literature, and the Káshi Khanda of the Skanda Purána may be considered as the store house of legends of Benares. But the Purános are among the latest of the shastras or sacred books, and have no historical value. One such legend may be here given as a specimen, in which

Pre-Buddhistic Period, up to 550 B. C.

the origin of the city is attributed to the creative power of Vishnu, exerted in honor of the great deity Shiva.

"The seven rishis approached Vishnu and desired to be shown the certain road to salvation. Vishnu, after some meditation, created a linga which shone in glorious effulgence. The linga at its birth was only a span wide but it gradually diffused itself till it covered space, its radius being panch kos (ten miles). This was Káshi. The world at this time was a collection of surging and heaving waters, and the linga stood unmoved on the surface of the deep. Vishnu, however arrived at the conclusion that the place was too small for the abode of the rishis, and consequently created the earth and placed it in juxtaposition to and surrounding the linga."

Legends of this character are readily accepted and implicitly believed in by the devout Hindu, and one may occasionally see in the temple courts crowds seated at the feet of some priest, and listening in rapt attention, while tales of this sort are read to them in sonorous Sanscrit.

There is a history hidden in the names of the city. Káshi, or Kási, as is well known, is the religious name of the city, although it is admitted that Benares, in its ancient form of Váránasi, is an older name. It is now apparently agreed that one of the earliest of the Hindu kingdoms, that of the Kásis, had Váránasi for a time at least, for its capital. The name of the rulers clung to their principal city after they themselves had passed into oblivion and in later times it has become, with an honorific affix, the name used by devout Hindus all over India, and *Káshi ji* whenever uttered awakens feelings of religious fervour in the minds of true believers.

It is probable that Benares is on the site of a considerable city founded or discovered by the Aryan invaders soon after they left the Punjáb, and, situated as it is, on a lofty bank overlooking the river with a sacred sangam, or river junction, north and south of it, very early grew into religious importance. Its situation also in the midst of an agricultural and therefore, wealthy and peaceable community, remote from the Himalayas in the north and the Vindhyas in the south, where wars with the aborigines so long persisted, must have tended to make it early the abode of the saint and the scholar, and the refuge of the devotee and pilgrim.

In all probability too Benares saw the rise of Brahmanism out of the old Vedic religion, for it was a great city when, according to Max Müller, the law of rite and ceremony in the Brahmanas, and the philosophic dreams of the Upanishads, were produced. Probably for over three thousand years the priest and philosopher have sat side by side in Benares, and together have elaborated that close woven web of faith and practice in which the Hindu mind is today enmeshed. The vision of that early past is dim, but enticing, and it floats before the eye like the picture in some magic crystal. When Babylon was an upstart state contending with lordly Nineveh, and the early Jewish heroes and kings were welding the Israelitish tribes into a nation; while the Phœnician barks were yet content to plough the sheltered Mediterranean not yet daring to attempt the white cliffs of Albion; while the Grecian communities were slowly and jealously forming themselves into commonwealths and Athens was hardly more than a name, and Rome not yet thought of, here in this quiet retreat, by the calm flowing Ganges and amid the teeming, fruitful plains, dwelt thoughtful seers and proud priests, and hither to worship at a hundred shrines toiled streams of wistful pilgrims. Things were then much as they are to-day and the gymnosophists, or naked philosophers, who amazed Alexander's soldiers were own brothers to Mrs. Steele's hero, "In the Permanent Way.'

But the priest predominated over the seer as the temples overshadowed the monasteries, and thus came about that great change in religious practice which indirectly gives us our first historical glimpse of Benares. There is no doubt that Gautama, called the Buddha, the sage of the Sákya tribe, headed a revolt against too much ceremony. A prince of the warrior caste, born a hundred miles north of Benares at Kapilavasthu, and enlightened at Gáya, a hundred miles to the south, he came to Benares about the middle of the sixth century B. C., about the time the Jews returned to Jerusalem from captivity. Thus Benares was in all probability not only the place where Hinduism was elaborated into Bráhmanism, but also the birth place of that other world religion, Buddhism. The mild and gentle teacher took up his abode at the Isipattana Vihâr, a monastery in a deer park to the north of the present city, now known as Sârnâth, where masses of broken brick and one solitary tower mark the place of former greatness and power.

Buddhistic Period
550 B. C.—750 A. D.

For a long time a spirit of tolerance seems to have marked both the old and the new sect for we know that both existed side by side for many centuries. The influence too of the great Buddhist monarch Asoka, who ruled at Patna not two hundred miles away, about 250 B. C., must have been powerfully felt here. Buddhist pilgrims from the lands further East to which the new faith had been carried found their toilsome way to the shrine of their faith, and two of them have helped to lift the veil on the past. The Chinese devotees, Fa Hian at the beginning of the 5th century and Hiouen Thsang in the 7th, came to obtain manuscripts of their scriptures, and fragmentary accounts of their travels are found in the Chinese classics. They found

Benares a great city with a wealthy and peaceful population, full of temples and statues of the gods, and crowded with devotees as to-day. "Families of very great wealth whose houses are stored with rare and precious things, are to be seen. The people are gentle and polished and esteem most highly men given to study." Of the devotees we read, "Some cut off the hair; others reserve a tuft upon the crown, go naked and are destitute of any kind of clothing. Some besmear their bodies with ashes." This was thirteen hundred years ago, and yet is a true picture of Benares to-day. Hiouen Thsang, pious Buddhist though he was, goes on to say that though "there are thirty (Buddhist) monasteries containing about three thousand devotees," yet, "there are a hundred temples of the Hindu gods and about ten thousand heretics," these last being evidently Hindus. Buddhism was then fast declining but its splendour was still great.

Out of all the magnificent temples, porches, chapels, monasteries, towers and statues that then met the pilgrims' eyes, and marked the power and wealth of Buddhism what now remains? As one stands on the mound of shattered bricks, under the shadow of the ruined tower of Sárnáth, Wren's proud epitaph comes to mind, but with how sad a meaning!

"Si monumentum quaeris, Circumspice."

Examine the carved face of that massive tower! Go to the bamboo grove at Bakariya Kund where, desecrated by alien tombs, stands a perfect specimen of a Buddhist temple! Observe the defaced columns and richly carved architraves of the old Buddhist portico now known as the mosque of the Ganj Shahid! Search the byways and alleys of the Mussulmán quarter to the north of the city for carved stones and forgotten shrines, and in these you will find all that is left of the mighty faith which once, for over a thousand years, rivalled and threatened to subdue Bráhmanism in Benares. Wiser men will say, "Not all!" and will point to certain modifications of Hindu belief and practice such as the absence of animal sacrifice and the existence of begging fraternities of monks, and will see in these and other things traces of that great spiritual revolt. But yet from India, as from Benares, Buddhism as a faith was banished by a determined and triumphant Brahmanic revival.

The Brahmanic Revival. 750-1000 A. D.

The suppression of Buddhism was followed by a period in which the great body of Buddhist believers were admitted to the ancient fold, and the people were once more bound together in one faith. There are few traces of this period in Benares itself though the florid designs of certain ancient temples, now in many cases turned into mosques, date from that period. The legend of the expulsion of King Devadása by the wiles of Ganesha, and the return of Shiva, may be an echo of that final victory. The very absence of any history indicates a period of quiet in which the city settled down to the old, or only slightly altered, order of things and resumed and extended its sway.

Muhammadan Period 1000-1700.

The Muhammadan invasions very soon began to affect Benares, for though it was far distant from the passes in the frontier through which the plundering hordes forced their way, tales of its wealth and sanctity aroused alike the cupidity and the fanaticism of the invaders. It is related that in 1018 Mahmud of Ghazni, on the ninth of his expeditions penetrated as far as Benares, defeated and slew the Rájput prince, Rájá Banár, and after razing to the ground his castle at Ráj Ghát, plundered and burnt the temples, and departed, leaving the city a shattered and smoking ruin. Nearly two centuries of comparative peace served to restore the glories of the sacred city, and then again in 1194 came Muhammad of Ghor, like his predecessor, to kill, to plunder and destroy. Mussulmán historians exultingly relate that at this time a thousand idolatrous temples were razed to the ground and fourteen hundred camels scarcely sufficed to carry away the spoil.

In the centuries that immediately followed this the Hindu learnt how to live with his masters. 'The sheep must live and for its life would not unwillingly spare a little wool,' and so, while their lords quarrelled and fought, and rival dynasties rose and fell, they deftly served the stronger side and, with that quiet tenacity of purpose so characteristic of the Oriental, they still moved along their accustomed way.

> The East bowed low before the blast,
> In silent deep disdain;
> It heard the legions thunder past,
> Then plunged in thought again.

Under the Mogul Emperors its fortunes varied. Large-hearted Akbar, who lived in "the spacious times of great Elizabeth," patronized and protected wise and devout men of all creeds. But his son and successor, Jehángir, by his own confession was guilty of one crowning act of vandalism in the destruction of the old Visveswar temple in the centre of the city. From the materials and on the site of that splendid shrine he erected the principal mosque, leaving, with a refinement of cruelty, some shattered fragments of the old temple built into the back of the mosque. True it is however that about the same time, Rájá Mán Singh, a Rájput chief in the service of the Emperor as Governor of Bengal, had influence enough to be allowed to add one edifice to the beauties of the city which remains to this day, the Mán Mandir, better known as the Observatory.

Dárá, grandson of Jehángir, has an interesting connection with the city. He was Governor of Bengal under his father Sháh Jehán and seems to have, for a time, resided in Benares where a mohalla, Dáránagar, is named after him. He seems to have been a man of a studious and tolerant temperament, and it is related that under his direction a translation of the Upanishads was made into Persian. This version was afterwards translated into Latin by one of the early Jesuit Missionaries, and in this form arrested the attention of the German philosopher Schopenhauer, by whom it was brought to the notice of European scholars; so that we may say that from Benares the stream of Eastern learning first found its way to Europe.

Under the fanatic Aurangzeb, the last of the Great Moguls, Benares was once more called to suffer, for during his reign many of the principal temples were destroyed and from the ruins of the chief of them was built that great Mosque, whose lofty minarets form the most striking object on the river bank. The crowning insult however was inflicted when the Emperor decreed a new name for the city, calling it Muhammadábád, a title, however, which the slow strong waves of time have washed away.

The Maráthas. 1700—1800

After Aurangzeb, indeed, during his time, sprang up that revival of Hindu patriotism of which the Maráthas headed by their chief Sivaji were the leaders. Slowly, as the old Mussulmán power receded, the patriotic wave advanced and brought wealth and honour to the old home of the faith. Under the Marátha influence Benares revived, and the chief of the present temples and other sacred buildings date from this period. Marátha princes and princesses vied with each other in pouring their gifts into the lap of the deified city. To this period is due the Anna Purná temple, the colonnade at the Gyán Bápi, the Golden temple, Bhaironáth and Trilochan temples, Munshi Ghát and Ahlya Baî Ghát.

It was at the end of the 18th century that Benares was ceded to the East India Company by Asaf-ud-daula, the nominal Emperor of Delhi, and from this time Benares became an integral part of the British Empire.

Under British Rule. 1800.

At the time of the cession, Rájá Cheit Singh, a Hindu vassal of the Emperor, was ruler of Benares, and he very soon came into conflict with the dominant power in the person of Warren Hastings.

In 1780 as a dependent of the East India Company and enjoying its protection and patronage, the Rájá had been called upon to support his masters in their struggle with France in the south. To these demands Cheit Singh had responded but tardily and when, in 1781, a fresh demand for a contingent of 1,000 horse was made, the Rájá refused point blank and was promptly fined 50 lacs of Rupees. or £ 500,000. To compel obedience and realize this enormous fine, Warren Hastings, in the rainy season of 1781, came up to Benares and encamped in Mádho Dás's garden, close to the present Prince of Wales' Hospital. Rájá Cheit Singh was at that time in his fort at Shiválá Ghát and, terrified at the near approach of Hastings, wrote several submissive letters, and when on the 16th of August two companies of sepoys commanded by three young English lieutenants were sent to arrest him, he willingly submitted. The fort was occupied and the Rájá confined in a suite of rooms overlooking the river, whose waters, swollen by the rains, lapped the walls just under his window. If the Rájá was submissive his followers were not, and very soon the fort was surrounded by a turbulent and threatening mob. Presently it became known that by a curious and as it proved, a fatal blunder, the sepoys were unprovided with ammunition, and on this, the assailants, encouraged by fresh relays of turbulent spirits from Rám Nagar, burst into the building and overpowered and finally massacred the whole contingent of two hundred and five sepoys with their officers. Cheit Singh was let down through one of the windows into a boat and, followed by the greater portion of his exulting rescuers, crossed to Rám Nagar.

The situation of Warren Hastings at this time, alone in a turbulent city, with a greatly reduced escort and in a practically unfortified garden was critical in the extreme, and there can be no doubt that he was only saved by the fatuous inaction of Cheit Singh and his followers, who persisted in remaining on the other side of the river at Rám Nagar. At last, however, they showed signs of a determination to make an attack on the garden, and Hastings decided on a retreat to Chunár Fort. This retreat was made at night and was, in Hastings' own words, "retarded and impeded by an incredible tumult of servants, palanquins and baggage of every description, which for a time threatened a total destruction of our march." Chunár, however, was reached in safety and although on the departure of the English the whole district blazed up in insurrection, Warren Hastings was back again in less than a month and with an iron hand soon restored order. Cheit Singh fled to Gwalior, leaving his estates forfeit in the hands of the English who bestowed them on his nephew Mahip Náráyan, from whom the present Mahá Rájá is descended.

The memorials of this event are to be sought for in three spots. At the back of the Shiválá Fort are the graves of the three lieutenants, carefully railed in and preserved. The following inscription is inscribed on a stone let into one of the tombs.

"This tablet has been erected by the Government N. W. P. to preserve the last earthly resting place of Lieut. Arch. Scott, 1st Battalion Sepoys, Jer. Symes, 2nd Battalion Sepoys, J. Stalker, Resd. Body Guard, who were killed Augst 17th, 1781, near this spot, doing their duty."

In Cheit Ganj, near the police station, is a walled enclosure, over the gate of which is a stone slab with the following inscription:—

"The Enclosed Ground was the burial place of Brave Men who died in the performance of their duty on the 16th of August, 1781 A. D. This wall was built to protect the spot from desecration, A. D. 1862."

This enclosure was the old city burial ground and in 1829, just after St. Mary's Church in Cantonments had been renovated and enlarged, the monuments and gravestones from this old burial ground (together with a number of bodies) were removed to the compound of St. Mary's by Mr. James Prinsep, at that time magistrate of Benares. Chief among the monuments then removed is a fine stone obelisk, standing on a square base, on the four sides of which may still be traced the following quaint and touching inscription:—

"*This Monument to the Memory of Lieut. John Stalker, Arch. Scott, and Jeremiah Symes, massacred at Sewálah on the 16th day of August, 1781, Though erected by the hand of Friendship shall offer no Praise which themselves might blush to read Yet be it remembered that the Determined Courage they shewed was not an Act of Despiration but a part of their character as British Officers that they fell not wholly useless to their Country's Cause in the Sentiments of Awe and Respect they impressed on their Enemies in the tears of Regret and Emulation they drew from their Fellow Soldiers.*"

Eighteen years after these events another crisis arose in the British occupancy of Benares, when the lives of brave men were again sacrificed, and when the indomitable courage of a single Englishman sufficed, not only to save the lives of many of his fellow countrymen, but also to preserve the supremacy of the Government whose servant he was. In 1799 British affairs in India were in a very critical condition. In the south, Tippoo Sultan was gathering his forces for that last struggle which ended in his overthrow and death at Seringapatam in May. The French, maddened by their crushing defeat by Nelson at the battle of the Nile, were doing all in their power to harry and weaken their rivals in India. In the north, a large Afghán army under Zamán Khán at Lahore was threatening a descent on the plains.

It was at this critical moment that the insurrection of Wazír Alí, the deposed Nawáb of Oude, occurred at Benares. Wazír Alí had in 1791 been appointed to succeed his reputed father as Nawáb of Oude but had within a year been deposed on the ground of illegitimacy, profligacy and general disaffection and sent to Benares, on the borders of his kingdom, where he lived in sulky retirement on a large pension. Ever since his deposition he had nursed the idea of revenge. He was only nineteen years of age and of the most arrogant temper and vicious habits. He never moved abroad without a large armed retinue, and disdained intercourse with all Europeans except Mr. Cherry, the British Resident at that time. From his residence in Mádho Dás's garden he kept up a correspondence with the Afghán army at Lahore, and had a whole circle of confederates at work concerting rebellion in the city and district. In several of the large houses in the city arms were collected, and at Pindrah Kot, a fortress fifteen miles outside Benares, a force was gathered to attack, at the favourable moment, the British troops encamped near by. The city was at that time in the most turbulent state. It was infested by a species of swaggering bully called Bánkás, so named from the peculiar curved dagger they carried, in the use of which they were very expert. These rogues lived on blackmail which they extorted from the more peaceable citizens, and were ready to join Wazír Alí or anyone else who could hold out to them promise of plunder. Early in January, when all their plans were laid and the conspirators were only waiting for the signal from the commander of the Lahore Army, there came an order from the Governor-General, through Mr. Cherry, that Wazír Ali should be immediately removed to Calcutta. Naturally the Wazír was deeply chagrined and discomfited, and determined on attempting a rising at once, hoping for revenge if not for success. On the 14th of January, 1799, he set out with his usual large retinue to visit Mr. Cherry, who then occupied the building now used as the Collector's kachaharí. On the way he met Mr. Davis, the Magistrate and his wife, mounted on an elephant returning from their morning ride. Wazír Alí's business was not with them just at that moment and so, after the usual salutations, they were allowed to pass, but not before Mr. Davis' sharp eye had detected something unusual in the number and array of the retinue. On his arrival at Mr. Cherry's house Wazír Alí was received in a friendly manner and offered a cup of tea, which he declined. Then, as Mr. Cherry continued his morning meal, he began in an angry tone to complain of the recent order and at last, suddenly jumping up, he seized Mr. Cherry and dealt him a blow with his dagger. This was regarded as the signal for action by his followers and the unfortunate man was immediately attacked from all sides. He managed however to break away from his assailants, but was followed and killed a few yards from the house. With him fell Mr. Evans, his secretary, and Captain Conway, who rode unsuspectingly up to the house while the disturbance was proceeding. The Wazír then collected his followers and moved off to Nandesar Kothí, the residence of Mr. Davis. On the way they met and killed in his palanquin Mr. Hill, who kept a shop in the city. In the meantime Mr. Davis, alarmed at the threatening aspect of Wazír Alí's retinue had immediately on his arrival home despatched a note of warning to Mr. Cherry, which however arrived too late. Being on the alert he saw the first of Wazír Alí's followers approach his house and fire on his servants. There was not a moment to be lost and, unable to get any other weapon, he snatched a spear from an attendant at the door and directed Mrs. Davis to ascend to the roof, taking with her the one child who remained below. The staircase they ascended was narrow and winding, and covered in at the top with a trap door of bamboo and matting. Over this Mr. Davis mounted guard to defend it, if possible, against this band of desperate men. The spear he had was no mean weapon. The shaft was of iron, plated with silver in rings to give a firm grasp, rather more than six feet in length and furnished with a long triangular blade of more than twenty inches, with sharp edges. The first man who attempted to make his way up the staircase was greeted with a sharp lunge of the spear, and hastily retreated with a badly wounded arm. The second, more wary, avoided the spear and grasping the blade with both his hands tried to wrest it out of Mr. Davis' hands, but he, dropping the shaft on the edge of the door and using it as a lever, tore it out of his assailant's hands which were severely cut by the sharp edges of the blade. After this no further attempt was made to force the stair, though many bullets were fired up the staircase and horsemen rode round the house on every side trying to get a shot at the occupants of the roof. Thus for nearly two hours, like another Leonidas at his Thermopylæ, did this brave man keep at bay a murderous band of two hundred desperadoes.

In the meantime the other Europeans had sought shelter, and one of them, Mr. Cleves, had, on a swift horse and by a circuitous route ridden to where, ten miles away, General Erskine's force was encamped. There he met with a troop of cavalry just returned from exercise and to their officer he communicated his news. The word of command was at once given and the force wheeled round and set off for Benares at a gallop. When the thunder of their hoofs was heard, Wazir Ali sullenly drew off his men and retired to his retreat in Madho Das's garden. Before night fell the garden had been attacked and Wazîr Alì forced to flee by unfrequented ways northwards to Azimgarh. For nearly a year he maintained himself in the wild country at the foot of the Himalayas, but he was eventually captured and the first anniversary of his unsuccessful rebellion saw him carried as a prisoner through Benares to Calcutta.

The lower portion of the staircase defended by Mr. Davis may still be seen in the Nandesar Kothi, and in the old cemetry at Chauka Ghat is a colossal monument to Mr. Cherry and his friends. It is in the form of a square pointed obelisk, set on an immense platform of stone ornamented at the four corners by large funeral urns. It has the following inscription which is of recent date:—

"This obelisk was erected in memory of
George Frederick Cherry, Esq., G. G.,s Agent.
Captain Conway.
Robert Graham, Esq.
Richard Evans, Esq.
Who were murdered by Wazir Ali, January 14th, 1799"

Benares maintained its reputation for being one of the most turbulent cities in India during the years that succeeded Wizir Ali's attempt at rebellion, but it was firmly and wisely governed and nothing of moment occurred till 1857—that ill-fated year—the year of the Sepoy revolt. Benares was the most easterly of the great cities where serious risings took place, and it was due entirely to the promptness and indomitable courage of the few Englishmen stationed here that the city was spared a scene of massacre such as took place in cities farther north. On Sunday, the 10th of May, the mutiny broke out at Meerut, and soon the great cities of the North-West, Delhi, Cawnpore, Lucknow, Bareilly, and Allahabad were wrapped in a blaze of rebellion. In five or six days the news reached Benares. At that time the military force stationed here consisted of three regiments of Native troops and a company of European Artillery. The whole of the European force amounted to less than 200 men, who had to watch over more than ten times their number of disaffected sepoys. All through May great uneasiness was felt, and at the end of the month incendiary fires in the native lines became frequent.

On the 4th of June came news of the mutiny of a Native Regiment at Azimgarh, sixty miles to the north, and it was rumoured that the mutineers were marching down to join their compatriots at Benares. Further delay was seen to be dangerous and it was decided early in the day to disarm the men next morning, but Colonel Neill, who had just arrived from Calcutta on his way to the front, counselled instant action. His advice was eventually taken and early in the afternoon of Thursday, the 4th of June, the troops were called out on parade. The little company of Englishmen with the battery of artillery in their midst, under the command of Brigadier Ponsonby, stood waiting to see what turn events would take. It seemed at first as if the men would obey the order to pile their arms for many of them did so, the English officers going amongst them and reasoning with them. But suddenly a panic seemed to seize them. The arms that had been laid down were snatched up and they commenced to fire on their officers. The guns were at once wheeled round and opened fire on the rebels, and in a short time they were in full flight. They were never allowed to re-form and before night the European settlement was in the hands of the English.

The European residents were accommodated in the Mint, a large building now belonging to the Mahárájá of Benares, where for several davs and nights in the most trying month of the year, and in constant fear of attack they remained huddled together in the utmost discomfort, while the city near at hand was bubbling and seething with insurrection. No organized attack however was made by the sepoys, and though on many occasions there was great danger and more than once seasons of panic were experienced, there was no actual loss of life or property, and when in September, Delhi was captured and Lucknow relieved the clouds began to lift and peace was restored.

The memorials of the mutiny in Benares are confined to the graves of the men who fell on the parade ground on the 4th of June. They may be found near the present barracks close to the Railway station, Only two have any mark attached, one being the grave of Lieut. Yorke Hayter of the 25th Bengal Native Infantry and the other of Captain Henry John Guise of the 13th Irregular Cavalry, who fell at the head of his men when charging the rebels. It is an interesting fact and one worthy of being remembered, that no single instance of unfaithfulness or treachery is reported to have occurred among the domestic servants of European residents in Benares during these troublous times.

CHAPTER III.

Present-day Benares.

"Forth fared they by the common way afoot
Seeing the glad and sad things of the town;
The painted streets alive with hum of noon,
The traders cross-legged, mid their spice and grain,
The buyers with their money in their cloth,
The war of words to cheapen this or that,
The shout to clear the road, the huge stone wheels,
The strong slow oxen and their rustling roads,
The singing bearers with their palanquins,
The broad-necked hamals sweating in the sun,
The house wives bearing water from the well
With balanced chatties, and athwart their hips
The black-eyed babes; the fly swarmed sweetmeat shop,
The weaver at his loom, the cotton bow
Twanging, the mill-stones grinding meal, the dogs
Prowling for orts * * *
Here a throng
Gathered to watch some chattering snake-tamer
Wind round his wrist the living jewellery
Of asp and nág, or charm the hooded death
To angry dance to drone of beaded gourd;
There a long line of drums and horns, which went
With steeds gay painted and silk canopies
To bring the young bride home; and here a wife
Stealing with cakes aud garlands to the god
To pray her husband's safe return from trade
Or beg a boy next birth; hard by the booths
Where the swart potters beat the noisy brass
For lamps and lotas; thence by temple walls
And gateways, to the river * * *

"The Light of Asia."

These lines, intended to describe the city of Ayodhyá more than two thousand years ago, might well be taken for a picture of every day life in Benares. In the variety and picturesque character of the scenes which meet the eye of the traveller as he wends his way through the narrow streets intersecting the almost solid block of masonry which forms the old city, Benares can certainly vie with any other city in India and outshine most.

But it is to Benares as a religious centre that Hindús from all over India wend their way as pilgrims year by year. It is impossible to convey any adequate idea of the intense feelings of veneration and affection with which the pious Hindú regards "Káshi ji" Let a Hindú regiment be marched through the district, and as soon as they cross the Pánch Kosí Road and enter the limits of the holy place, they rend the air with cries of "Káshi ji ki Jai! Jai! Jai." "Káshi beloved! Victory to thee! Victory! Victory!" The weary pilgrim, scarcely able to stand with age and weakness, blinded by the dust and heat and almost dead with fatigue, crawls out of the oven-like railway carriage and as soon as his feet touch the ground he lifts up withered hands and utters the same pious exclamation. Let a European in some distant city in casual talk in the bazar mention the fact that he has lived at Benares, and at once, voices will be raised to call down blessings on his head; for a "Kashí báshí," a dweller in Benares, is of all men most blessed. It is this peculiar sanctity of Benares which gives it the pre-eminence over every other city in India in the eyes of Hindus. Other cities may have famous shrines such as are to be found at Puri in Orissa, Prayág (Allahabad), Hardwár, Bindháchal, &c., but within the boundary of the Pánch Kosi Road every inch of Benares is holy ground to the pilgrim, and the spiritually enlightened see glories upon glories in her narrow streets, where the uninitiated suffer from foul sights and fouler smells.

Though Benares was the home and school of the later Vedic worship it so far exemplifies the progress of religion in India as to be now the shrine of the Puránic deities. Among its philosophers and thinkers of the modern school there may be those who desire to return to the primeval faith, but in its temples and throughout the whole public worship of the city the later deities hold sway. Each of the persons of the Puránic Trinity receives divine honours and, singularly enough, the city typifies the Indian people in the degree of honour rendered to each of these Gods. Shiva holds the first place, under the name of Mahádeva, followed closely by Vishnu as Krishna or Ráma, while Brahmá is hardly recognized.

The whole city is regarded as the special and peculiar domain of Shiva, whose ensign, a gilt trident or a perforated disc, flashes from the pinnacles of a thousand temples, and his emblem, the linga, and vehicle, the bull, surpass in number the inhabitants themselves. In honour of him, naked devotees, adorned by horizontal lines on forehead, arms and breast made from the grey ashes of cow-dung, crowd the river bank and infest the narrow streets and are regarded by the common people almost as re-incarnations of the great God and venerated as such. The Magistrate of Shiva, Bhaironáth resides in one of the richest of the temples in the city, and his magic staff is supposed to perambulate the city to punish offences at the bidding of its master.

Vishnu holds a nearly equal, but yet a subordinate place to Shiva in the affections of the inhabitants of Benares. His worshippers are distinguished by two perpendicular lines on the forehead, aud marks of his footprints are found in several parts of the city. The chief of the Vishnu temples is the Gopál Mandir, which is so jealously guarded that I have been unable to discover that any European has ever been allowed to enter its sacred precincts. Vishnu is the more homely, sociable deity of the triad, and as such finds a warmer place in the affections of Hindûs than the austere and mysterious Shiva, whose province it is to control human destiny in birth and death.

Brahmá, the first member of the Hindù triad, is strangely neglected in worship, and images of him are very scarce and when he is mentioned in legend and story he is usually represented as the minister and servant of Shiva.

In addition to those three deities a vast multitude of others hold the superstitious Hindu in awe. They are frequently ministers of the great ones as Hanumán, Bhairo, Nárad; or their children as Ganesh, Kártikeya, Saraswati; or their female counterparts as Párbati, Durgá, Káli, Sitá; or they are natural objects as the Sun, Suraj; the Moon, Somá; the Planets Navagraha; the Ganges, Gangá; while plants and trees, wells and tanks, and animals such as the crocodile, monkey, dog and cow are all objects of worship.

But idolatry does not confine itself even within these wide limits. There are seasons when almost every natural object is worshiped, when the farmer worships his plough, the tailor his needle, the carpenter his adze and chisel, and the clerk his pen, indeed with his strong pantheistic ideas the Hindu sees God in all things, and any accident may temporarily or permanently locate Him in a person or object.

But it is when divine honours are paid to erring human beings that idolatry reaches its lowest point, and in submitting to Brahmin worship the Hindu has rivetted on his own neck an iron yoke which has either rendered impossible or else terribly hindered all progress, and which only after the most painful struggles can be thrown off. Benares is the Brahmin's paradise.

They constitute nearly one-eighth of the city population. They line the river banks and infest the temples, where they sit like spiders watching for their prey. Their emissaries are abroad, travelling by railway to distant cities to promote pilgrimages and hover about the entrances to the city, to make sure of the unwary devotee. From father to son and to son's son the lucrative calling is handed on, and every umbrella on the Ganges shades a valuable hereditary property, concerning the succession to which there may be much heart-burning, and possibly a law suit before an English judge. It is impossible to over-estimate the effect of this evil system on the worshippers. Formal religion means formal ethics, and when the gravest sins may be condoned by a gift to the Brahmins, by the performance of a pilgrimage or at most by the erection of a temple, what wonder that Hindus should be famous for the almost utter absence among them of any adequate sense of sin.

But even Benares cannot stand still in this age of progress. The Railway, the Post, and the Telegraph have had their effect in widening the area of men's knowledge and opportunities, and a class of men is steadily growing who regard with contempt and a growing impatience, the ignorant folly of the mass of their nation, and who are seeking for some plan of deliverance. English education has opened the eyes of many to the gross ignorance of their spiritual superiors, and the translation into English of the Indian classics has done more to destroy the old unreasoning reverence for the Sanscrit books than almost anything else. The study of Sanscrit is admitted on all hands to be distinctly declining, and the day is not far distant when it will hold the same place in education in India as Hebrew does in Europe.

But Brahminism is almost Protean in its power to assimilate new ideas and adapt itself to new forms of worship, so that graduates from the English Colleges may often be found among the priests of these unclean temples, just as the post office savings bank is a convenient receptacle for the monthly takings at the ghât.

During the last few years competent observers declare that the number of pilgrims to Benares has increased, owing no doubt to the increased facilities of travel and the opening of the great Dufferin Bridge. The visitor may find here many new temples, some of them rivalling and even surpassing the old shrines in beauty and the costliness of their adorning. One of these, erected by the late Mahárájá of Benares, may be seen at Godaulia not far from Dasaswâmedh Ghát, the carving of which in parts is little short of exquisite. A second even more beautiful is near Durgâ-Kund. A third, adorned with a large number of gilded points is at Laksá, and a fourth, not so ornate, but yet, no mean structure, is at Chauká Ghât, near the iron bridge over the Barnâ.

But the revival, if so it may be called, is devoid of the marks of a movement towards better and nobler things. The new shrines show no progress in architecture, no development in design. The ritual is as stereotyped and formal as ever. The end aimed at in their erection is the old one, to perpetuate a name and to secure merit for the builder. A curious aspect of this movement is open to the visitor who cares to pay a visit to a stone mason's yard at the head of Dasaswâmedh Ghât, where temples great and small, plain and ornate, according to the taste and pocket of the purchaser are manufactured. Here they may be found, the pieces carved and numbered and fitted, complete even to the little brass trident at top, ready to be packed up and set down wherever the buyer may find it fit or possible.

Never before surely, was a system of religion found

more easy for the worshipper and more lucrative for the priest, which claims such august sanctions and threatens such dire perils, so comfortable for the idle and vicious rich, so oppressive to the honest, industrious poor, which promises so much and gives so little.

CHAPTER IV.

Alphabetical List of Places and Objects of Interest.

The following list has been prepared to enable the visitor to find readily the description of any place which he may observe, and the name of which he may hear. Usually the native name has been kept, but in one or two cases, such as the Monkey Temple and the Golden Temple, the English name, as being the more common one, has been used.

Anna Purna or Cow Temple. This is situated in the narrow lane which passes the front of the Golden Temple. It is sacred to Anna Púrná, the Goddess who "fills with grain" and who is supposed to have undertaken the task of feeding the inhabitants of the city. On one occasion, finding the task an unusally heavy one, she became very anxious about her clients. The Goddess Gangà (Ganges), however, generously promised to supply each applicant with a brass vessel full of water if she would add a handful of pulse. The labour thus happily divided, the people of Benares are now supposed to be in no fear of want. In the temple are kept large numbers of cows whose presence does not add to the cleanliness of the shrine. These are particularly sacred animals, and worshippers may often be seen kissing their tails and shewing other signs of reverence. Here too sit a great company of blind, halt and lame, and not a few sturdy vagabonds, who reap a good harvest from the indiscriminate alms of the worshippers. The Temple was erected in 1725 by a Rájá of Poona. It is surrounded by a covered verandah were devotees are to be seen seated, sometimes reading and explaining the sacred books to groups of attentive pilgrims. In one corner is an image of Ganesh, in another, one of Hanumân, in a third, Gauri Shankar with a stone box in front of her to receive gifts of grain and money, and in the fourth corner is an image of the sun in a chariot drawn by seven horses.

Close to the door of this temple is a figure of Ganesh, with silver face and hands, who receives great attention from passing worshippers notwithstanding his most grotesque appearance.

Near by is the Temple of Sanichar.

Arhai Kangura Mosque. Those interested in ancient remains, especially of Buddhism, will do well to pay a visit to this mosque which lies to the left of the main road beyond Machaudri Tank. The mosque is one of the finest in Benares, and entrance is obtained to it by a large stone gateway somewhat dilapidated. Passing through this gateway we find ourselves in a large courtyard, faced by a massive stone building consisting of a central chamber, capped by a dome, and two wings each two stories high, in which is a profusion of square stone columns of undoubtedly ancient origin. There is no doubt that this is a remnant of ancient Hinduism and probably of Buddhism. A stone slab was discovered in the building with a Sanscrit inscription containing a date equivalent to 1191 A. D. a date just previous to the invasion of Muhammad of Ghor. It seems probable that Buddhists, Hindus and Muhmmadans have in turn used the same materials, and that in this remarkable building there are preserved memorials of all these religions.

Near by, close to the Kashi Railway Station, are the Buddhist remains of the Ganj Shahid Mosque.

Bakariya Kund. This is an ancient tank lying a little to the right of the road which leads to Ráj Ghât from the Cantonments, and is famous for the Buddhistic remains which surround it. On the western side of the tank are the remains of a magnificent terrace, now unfortunately over-grown with shrubs, amongst which, however, may be found large numbers of beautifully carved stones. On the east few remains exist. On the north side is a large ghât surmounted by a building now used as a Muhammadan residence, the pillars of which, however, are plainly remnants of a building of Buddhistic origin. But the most perfect specimen of Buddhistie architecture to be found here, and in many ways the most interesting to be found in the whole of Benares, lies a little to the north-west of the tank picturesquely placed in the midst of a grove of feathery bamboos. It is a small Buddhist temple, crowned by a dome by the Muhammadans who have made use of it as a mausoleum. The building is supported by forty-two square pillars and is approached by three porticos. It is remarkable for its simplicity and strength, and the absence of ornamentation does not detract from, but rather enhances, the impression produced on the spectator. It seems certain that Bakariyá Kund was once the site of a very extensive Buddhistic religious settlement, consisting of terraces, cloisters, and temples surrounding the great central tank.

Bara Ganesh Temple. This temple of the Great Ganesh lies a little to the left of the main road just beyond Mádho Dás's garden. It is a temple held in high respect in Benares as will be manifest from its appearance, as also from the marble tablet near the door requesting "Gentlemen not connected with Hindú religion" not to enter the temple. The great figure of Ganesh, with silver hands and feet, and a gold aureole may be seen from the main doorway.

The present temple is a comparatively new structure having been built about fifty years ago, but certain of the images are evidently very old. The outer walls of the temple are decorated with a fresco of rats of all sizes and colours. These are the horses of Ganesh, and are fit emblems of the sly cunning for which the deity is famous. The story of how Ganesh became possessed of his elephant's head is differently told, but the following is the most common account :—

Ganesh was the first-born of Shiva and Párbatí, and on one occasion when going to bathe during the absence of her husband, Párbatí stationed the lad outside the door to prevent the entrance of intruders. Shiva returning, as was not uncommon with him, intoxicated with bhang, was refused admittance by his son who did not recognise him. Enraged at his impudence, the father [smote off his son's head. Párbatí hearing the scuffle rushed out and was overwhelmed with grief at the sight. Her husband, seeing his mistake, ordered the first head that could be found to be brought to him. This happened to be an elephant's, which he immediately clapped on to the shoulders of the boy, and so restored him. Párbatí, not over-pleased with the transformation, was comforted by the promise that her son should be worshipped first of all gods, which is literally true, as a figure of Ganesh adorns the entrance of nearly every temple, and also is placed over the main entrance of Hindú houses, and these are usually so low that he who enters must peforce bow his head, and so seem at least to do reverence to the deity.

Near by is the Jain Temple.

Barna Sangam. This is the name given to the junction of the Barná with the Ganges. All such junctions of rivers are sacred to the Hindú, and on this spot is a group of temples and shrines of some interest. The most important is a temple to Vishnu under the name of Adkesav. It is a handsome stone building at the head of the ghât leading down to the Barnâ, and rests on ten pillars of stone. Inside is an image of Vishnu with a black face surmounted by a silver crown. The image has four hands, also silver. The upper right hand holds a conch, the lower a lotus, the upper left hand has the sacred disc, and the lower a mace. In front of the door of the shrine is a stone with two feet rudely carved on its surface. These are said to be foot marks of Vishnu. A similar stone is to be seen at Manikarnikâ Ghât. The temple below the one just described is sacred to Sangameswar, which is only another name for Shiva, who is regarded as the Lord of this spot. Near by, in a crevice, is an image of Brahmâ with four heads. This is very unusual, for Brahmâ, on account of his incest with his daughter, Saraswatí, is very little worshipped in India. In this one spot, however, all the three members of the Hindu Triad, Brahmâ, Vishnu, and Shiva, are found together.

Near by is the Plateau of Râj Ghât.

Bhaironath Temple. This temple is situated in a lane leading from the main road near the Visweswar Ganj market. It is placed in a mass of buildings under the shade of an immense tamarind tree, which forces itself through the walls of the surrounding houses and spreads its feathery branches far and wide above them. Baironâth is the divinely appointed Kotwâl, or police magistrate of Benares, and through him the great god Shiva rules his capital. Bhaironâth rides on a dog, and thus traverses the city, making himself familiar with every creek and corner of it, and punishing all evil doers with the enormous staff which he carries. The temple resembles in general appearance other Benares temples, except that the dome is covered with a large number of gilded knobs. Inside the temple is a stone figure of the deity with a silver face and four hands. Offerings are made to him of flowers and native liquor. Worshippers, after presenting their offerings, are gently tapped by the presiding priest with a bundle of peacock feathers, this being the equivalent of a blow from the terrible club of the god. On the left of the entrance to the temple is a large stone figure of a dog, and on each side is a figure of an attendant bearing a large mace, while over the doorway are depicted the ten incarnations of Vishnu. The present building was erected in 1825, by a Maráthá Prince, Báji Rao of Poona. An ancient shrine previously existed here, some of the old images of which may be seen under a verandah on the south side of the temple. Close by is the temple of Dandpán.

Briddhkal Temple. This is one of the oldest temples in Benares, and is situated at the head of the lane running north from the Visweswar Ganj market. The temple is famous for a well and a small reservoir the water of which is said to have the power of not only curing all diseases, but of bestowing long life on all who bathe in it. The temple is a very dilapidated building and consists of several courtyards, all of which, except the central one in which the well is situated, show signs of great neglect. Facing the visitor on the left as he enters is a large stone figure of Hanumán, the monkeygod, raddled over in the usual style. To the right of this is the well, and in front of that and in the centre of the courtyard is a shallow octagonal pool, full of the foulest water imaginable, consisting, as it does, of the drippings from the well. This is the water which is said to possess the miraculous properties of healing disease and prolonging life. It is probable that instead of decreasing, it is the cause of spreading disease, for people afflicted with almost all the ills that flesh is heir to bathe in this stagnant pool, of which the water is rarely changed. Around the well may be observed a large number of small rooms containing images of various deities, the chief of which are emblems of Shiva. The legend attached to the temple is to the effect that it was built by a certain Rájá Márkanda, whose devotions during a period of sickness were so remarkable that Mahádeva not only healed him but made him young again. The Rájá, out of gratitude, built this temple and gave it the name which it now bears, and which consists of two words meaning "old" and "death." Mahádeva still further pleased with this evidence of piety endowed the well with the miraculous properties which it is still supposed to possess.

Close to Briddhkal, a few yards to the west, is the small shrine of Alpmriteswar, the god who delivers those who are at the point of death.

Buddhistic Remains. These are to be sought for at Sàrnàth, the Arhai Kangura Mosque, Bakariyà Kund, Làt Bhairo, the Gyàn Bàpi Mosque, and Ganj Shahid Mosque.

Dandpan Temple. This temple is very near the Bhaironáth Temple, and here may seen what is said to be the veritable truncheon of Bhaironáth. It is a stone shaft, four and a half feet in height, with a carved top. It is usually decorated with garlands and copiously sprinkled with Ganges water. This staff is said to be so intelligent that at the command of its master, it, of its own motion, proceeds to punish offenders by terrible blows. In the wall of the temple is a small shrine containing a very realistic image of the goddess Kálí. In this temple may also be seen the famous Kál Kúp or Well of Fate. It is an ordinary well, but so situated that the light falls into it from a square hole in the wall above. This produces a peculiar reflection in the water below, such that the spectator sees his face, framed as in a picture, deep down at the bottom of the well. This reflection can always be seen so long as the sun shines, but on cloudy days it is more or less indistinct. Woe then to the hapless wight who, on looking into this well, fails to make out his own face, for his doom is fixed, and in six months at the longest he must die. The only comfort to him is that under the some roof, and near the well, is an image of Mahá Kál, or Great Fate, who will, if propitiated, save him from evil in the world to come.

Ganj Shahid Mosque. This Mosque is a long low building close to the city entrance of the Káshi Railway Station, and takes its name from the large number of Mussulmán soldiers who are reputed to have fallen in the seige of the ancient fort of Rájá Banár, and who were buried here. The name means "the Treasure House of Martyrs." The mosque consists of two cloisters, one of which is about a foot and a half lower than the other, the roof of both being supported by a large number of beautifully carved stone pillars. In the smaller there are thirty pillars, each being a little less than nine feet in height. The larger cloister has forty pillars, ten feet in height, larger and more beautifully carved than those in the smaller cloister. These pillars are joined above by architraves of stone all of which, with the exception of one or two recent additions, are beautifully carved. The carving on some of the large pillars is exquisite, and even after being plastered with successive coats of white-wash the work is still very sharply defined. In the centre of the large cloister is an erection now used as a pulpit by the Mullah, or Mussulmán preacher, but a little examination will suffice to show that it is really the old Sinhásan, or throne of Buddha. The canopy over this throne is very beautifully carved. It is very probable that a third cloister, similar to the smaller one, formerly joined the larger, thus making one long covered room, of which the Sinhásan occupied the centre. It will be observed that the ceiling of this building is in places of a dark brown, almost black, colour. This is due to the fact that in 1857, when barracks for European troops were erected on the plateau near by, this entire building was used as a vast cook-house. It must be remembered that the back wall is not a part of the original building, and the stone floor is a recent addition.

Ghats, The. The magnificent series of stairs and buildings which line the left bank of the Ganges forms the chief feature of the sights of Benares. Mr. W. S. Caine, M. P., is not too enthusiastic when in his "Picturesque India" he says, "Viewed from the river, Benares presents a panorama of palaces, temples and mosques, surmounted by domes, pinnacles, and minarets, stretching three miles along the top of the bank. From these descend great flights of stone stairs broken into wide platforms, on which are built exquisite Hindu shrines, bathing houses, and preaching canopies. Ghàts, platforms, and piers are alive with pilgrims from every part of India, in every variety of custume and every stage of dress and undress, grouped under large straw umbrellas, sitting at the feet of some learned mahant or preacher, gazing at holy ascetics, jostled by sacred bulls, crowding in and out of the water, drying themselves with towels, prostrate at the margin telling beads. Every morning during his stay in Benares, the European traveller should take a boat and row slowly down in front of the ghàts."

The ghàts have been described in this list not in alphabetical order, but in the order in which they actually occur along the river bank. Starting from Dasaswamedh Ghàt the traveller should proceed *up* the stream, and after he has gone as far as he chooses, should return to the same point, and go *down* the river.

Dasaswamedh Ghat. This is the central ghát of the city, and is one of the most famous in Benares, being one of the five specially holy places on the river bank. The other four are Assi Sangam, Manikarniká Ghát, Pánch Gangá Ghát and Barná Sangam. To visit these spots in due succession and with appropriate offerings is to perform the *Pánch-tírth*, an act of piety of no mean efficacy. This ghàt is a good example of the double use of such places, *i. e.* as a quay for the landing of goods and passengers, and as a convenient spot for religious bathing. Here great quantities of stone from Mirzapur and Chunar, for building and other purposes, are landed, as well as cargoes of wood for fuel, and fodder for cattle, while next to Manikarniká, by far the largest concourse of bathers may be observed here.

The name of the ghát embodies a curious legend. Hither, in the days when the devout Rájá Devadása was in possession of the city, and all the motley troop of gods and goddesses, who, with Shiva at their head now hold rule here, were in exile, came Brahmá as a spy of the outcasts, to discover some way of ousting the Rájá and recovering possession of the sacred spot. Arriving on his sacred goose, he adopted the garb of the Brahmin ascetic, and wandered with delight among the temples, and along the sacred ghàts of the city. In order to achieve his end it occurred to him to entrap the devout Rájá in some heinous sin, and so, with the customary assurance of a Brahmin, he demanded the materials for a great sacrifice. The Rájá delighted, provided enough for ten, and to Brahmá's confusion, as he scrupulously examined the materials provided, he found nothing was missing, not one leaf, not one petal of a sacred flower, everything, to the ten sacred horses, was there. With great pomp then, under Brahmá's direct superintendence, the solemn rite was performed, and henceforth the spot was made sacred in the highest degree, being equal in merit to Prayág (Allahabad) where the sacred Gangá and Jamná join. From this circumstance comes the name, *dasa*—ten, *aswa*—horse, *medna*—sacrifice.

The curious may be interested in knowing how Rájá Devadása (in whom we have probably some dim memory of a pious Buddhist ruler, who for a time repressed idolatry) was at last dethroned. The faithless Brahmá never returned, so Ganesh, the sly, the crafty Ganesh, creeping hither by sewer and kennel on his rat, took the form of a Brahmin, and asked an audience of the Rájá. His well-feigned air of profound piety soon acquired for him the post of spiritual director to Devadása, and when asked to point out to his pupil some method of still higher spiritual achievement, he promised him enlightenment in a dream. In that dream came the command to leave Benares, with its holy pomp and ease of calm devotion, and trust to the will of God. The faithful Rájá obeyed, and when once outside, Ganesh resumed his true form; Shiva and his unholy troop re-entered in triumph and have never since been ejected.

At the southern end of the ghát is a low white-washed building quite devoid of architectural beauty, which is the temple of *Sítalá*, the goddess of small-pox. The goddess is represented by an old stone, rudely carved into the semblance of a human figure and set in a niche covered by a brass screen. The temple is frequented by large numbers of women, and at times when small-pox rages in the city, which is not an unfrequent occurrence, processions are made to the temple, and special offerings presented to propitiate the diety. In the same building is a large lingam in a brass socket, which has raised figures of snakes upon it. This is Dasaswámedheswar, the presiding deity of the ghát. Behind the temple is a pair of stone figures representing Rádhá and Krishna. A little further along, and visible from the river, are six life size figures in niches. The first three in order from right to left are, Gangá, the Ganges, riding on a crocodile, Saraswatì, the wife and daughter of Brahmá, and Jamná the sacred river, here shown as a goddess. The other three in the same order are Vishnu, the Trìmùrti, an attempt to shew Shiva, Vishuu, and Brahmá in one, and Narsingh, the lion-man incarnation of Vishnu.

Ahalya Bai Ghat. The stately ghàt next in order to Dasaswamedh was built by Ahalya Bai, a famous Maráthá princess who from 1766 to 1795 ruled Indore. She was a woman of remarkable powers of mind and was also deeply religious. This ghat furnishes an indication of the way in which Benares has been enriched by the religious bounty of the Maráthás. She also had a share in the construction of the Lolárik Kuán and the temples which adorn the river's edge at Manikarniká Ghát.

Munshi Ghat. This is in many way the most remarkable, as it is the most imposing in appearance of all the ghâts. The two massive pilasters of stone which front the river, and the exquisite little chambers, beautifully carved, which adorn the very summit of this lofty building, give it an appearance of grace which is equalled by no other ghát on the river side. It was built by the Dewán of Nágpore, Srì Dhar Naráyan Dás, between 1812 and 1824, but has been recently purchased by the Rájá of Darbhanga.

Rana Ghat or Rana Mahal. This is an old building and somewhat dilapidated. It was built in the 17th century by the Mahárána of Udaipur, belonging to one of the oldest lines of native rulers in India.

Chausathi Ghat is so named from a temple of Chausathi Devi, at the head of the flight of stairs. The ghát was built by Rájá Digapatti of Bengal.

Pande and Sarbeshwar Ghats are almost deserted. The only sign of life and inteıest remaining is a Brahmin who still clings to these spots and with difficulty colleots a few copper coins.

Raja Ghat. This ghát, with the temples above, was erected by Rájá Vináyak Ráo, Peshwá of Chitrakot. The lofty building above is inhabited by Brahmins, and for the repair of this building, and the feeding of the residents, a large sum of money was bequeathed by the Rájá and invested in Government securities.

Narad Ghat is so named after the famous Rishi. It is a very picturesque ghát. At the top, the steps wind to the right and are shaded by two magnificent peepul trees. At the head of the ghát is a small shrine sacred to Náradeswar.

Mansarwar Ghat consists of nothing but a flight of steps which lead to Mánsarwar Kund in the lane above. The ghát was erected by the Rájá Mán Sing of Jaipur, who also built the Mánmandir Ghát.

Someswar Ghat is named from a temple to Soma, the moon, which is found at the head of the ghát.

Chauki Ghat is remarkable for the large collection of stone idols which are placed on a raised platform surrounding the base of the large peepul at the top of the Ghát. Many of these are figures of Nág, the serpent deity.

Kidar Ghat. This is one of the finest gháts on the Ganges, and is said to be the loftiest. The ghát consists of several flights of stairs which lead up to the famous Kidár Temple, the most important shrine in the Bengali quarter. At the top of the first flight of steps is a square tank called *Gauri Kund* in honor of Gauri, one of the names of the wife of Shiva. It is claimed for the foul water with which this tank is filled, that it has the power to cure fever. On the steps of the ghát will be observed a number of emblems of Shiva, some of them of very large size and all decorated with offerings of flowers and rice.

The temple of *Kidárnáth* may be here described as it is most accessible from the river bank. Kidarnath is another name for Shiva to whom the temple is dedicated. The guardians of the temple are very precise and will not admit visitors wearing shoes, but the chief objects of interest may be seen from the doorway. The temple consists of a central square building, or shrine, surrounded by a colonnade in which are several small shrines containing a collection of idols, two only of which are of any size or importance. They are of brass and are kept screened from public view by cloths, which are only removed by the attendant Brahmin on the receipt of a gratuity. Around the colonnade are seated a multitude of beggars who spread out their dirty clothes and whine for alms from the worshippers. The central shrine contains the usual emblem of Shiva, and is lit by a multitude of small lamps. The most remarkable feature of the temple is the two statues in black stone which guard the entrance to the shrine. They are six feet in height and beautifully executed. Each has four hands, one of which holds a trident, another a club, a third a flower, and the fourth is upraised and held on a level with the breast in an attitude as if demanding silence and attention. These figures are called Dwárpáls, or doorkeepers.

Lali Ghat consists of a narrow flight of steps, said to have been erected by a certain Láli Dás. It is also called Chintámuni Ghát, which is a designation of Ganesh, a figure of whom occupies a prominent place on the lower steps.

Mashan Ghat. This is merely a landing place and is marked by a stone erection, on the top of which is a lingam called Masháneshwar. At this ghát occasional cremations take place and local tradition has it that this is the original Burning Ghát of Benares, and that the first Domra was a son-in-law of Shiva.

Hanuman Ghat is a handsome flight of steps, at the head of which is a temple of Hanumán, the monkey god. The stone building at the head of the ghát was recently very thoroughly repaired by the devotees who reside there, and who collected funds for the work from the Hindus.

Dandi Ghat is remarkable, as its name implies, for the number of devotees who frequent it, and whose distinguishing feature is the dandá, or wand, which they carry. Along the edge of the lower flight of steps may be seen the little round holes in which these wands are stuck while the owners are bathing.

Shivala Ghat is a magnificent building once used as a fort by Cheit Singh, Rájá of Benares. For an account of the tragic occurrences which have made this fort famous the visitor is referred to chapter II of this book. The fort is now inhabited by the descendants of the Mogul Emperors, who are in receipt of a pension from government. The large cluster of buildings adjoining the fort to the north is a *Hindú Monastry,* in which a number of monks reside. From this place they set out to perform their devotions at the various shrines in the city, and to obtain their food, either by voluntary doles (they never beg) or at the various places in the city, where rich Hindús acquire merit by feeding the devout. The ghát is continued for some distance southwards by a massive stone pushta, or rampart, strengthened by octagonal pilasters. Above it is a long stone building in which reside the royal pensioners above referred to.

Bachraj Ghat. The next ghát to Shiválá is peculiar as being the property of the Jain sect. The property was acquired by purchase from the builder whose name still attaches to it. The three temples above, with their gilded pinnacles and pendant bells, belong to this sect, which, though not numerous, is yet very influential on account of the wealth of its members. The more northern section of the ghát is nearly new, being only some thirty years old; the southern part is a hundred years older.

Janki Ghat is quite new, having been erected within the last ten years by the Ráni of Sursand whose Benares residence crowns the top of the steps. The four Shiva temples, whose resplendent gilded pinnacles may be seen from the river, are within the precincts of the Ráni's palace. Just below Jánki Ghát is the pumping station of the Benares Water-works. Benares has the honor of being the first city to be supplied with water direct from the sacred stream, and this fact conduces in no mean degree to the popularity among the native population of the water supply.

Tulsi Ghat. This forms the first section of the row of stone buildings which fittingly concludes the long array of Gháts towards the south. The house which crowns and overlooks the ghát is said to have been the residence of Swámi Túlsi Dás, the writer of the Hindi version of the famous epic of the Rámáyan, so popular throughout North India. Certain relics of the poet are still exhibited, such as an old pair of shoes, a chair, &c., but it is very improbable that they ever belonged to the Swámi. Túlsi Dás was a contemporary of our own Shakespeare, and the ghát certainly has an ancient appearance though it is very improbable that it is as old as it is claimed to be,

Baji Rao Ghat. This is a continuation of Túlsi Ghát and was the work of the last of the Maráthá Peshwás of Poona. The building is unfinished and neglected. The rooms situated in the handsome carved gallery which overlooks the river are occupied by wandering sanyásis.

Lala Misr Ghat. This is a handsome stone building with multiple round pilasters at either end, and crowned by a gallery protected by lattice work. It was built by a wealthy merchant whose name it still bears, but is now the property of the Rájá of Rewa. This is the last building in the series.

Assi Sangam Ghat, at the point where the Assi joins the Ganges, is a very sacred spot although there is no building to mark it. It is one of the five most sacred places on the river bank and is visited first by pilgrims who perform the Pánch-tìrth pilgrimage.

The visitor should now return to Dasaswámedh Ghát, from which point the description of the northern Ghâts begins.

Manmandir Ghat. This is the next ghàt to Dasawamedh *down* the river *i. e.* northwards, indeed it is from the steps of this ghát that the traveller usually embarks. The ghát and the building above, once a residence, now an observatcry, were erected less than 300 years ago, by Rájá Mán Singh of Jaipur, Governor of Bengal under Akbar the Great, and is in all probability the oldest building on the river bank. As seen from the river the building has a striking appearance, and attention should be specially directed to the very delicate stone carving of the balcony at the northern end of the building, overlooking the ghát. Mr. Prinsep says of this balcony, "It may have belonged to a more ancient building before being set up in its present position by Rájá Mán Singh, but whether executed or borrowed by him, it bears away the palm of antiquity in the town, and is a chef d'oeuvre of its kind."

Fergusson in his "Oriental Architecture" says that the same Raja erected a temple at Bindraban in which there is a balcony very similar to this one. Now, as we know that the old Visveswar temple, destroyed by Jehangir was erected by this same Raja and that he was in all probability alive at the time of its destruction, it is just possible that this balcony was part of the old temple and was rescued by its owner and placed here.

At the top of the ghát and under the shade of the wide spreading peepul tree, which greatly adds to the picturesque appearance of the spot, is a collection of idols and shrines. The chief of these is the temple of *Dálbhyeswar*. The deity is only another form of the protean Shiva, and his symbol is placed at the bottom of a stone cistern some distance below the level of the floor. The deity is credited with the power of producing rain, and in the hot season is copiously bathed with water from the Ganges. Should the much needed rains be delayed the cistern is filled to the brim and the deity entirely immersed, when it is supposed rain will infallibly ensue. The idol is also called the *Poor Man's Friend,* and is supposed to give material prosperity to his worshippers, though there is little evidence of the fact forthcoming.

Mir Ghat is a simple flight of stone steps leading up to the Dharm Kúp and a group of temples near it. Near the base of the ghât may be observed several erect stones marking the site of Suttee. These may be observed at several spots on the bank but more especially here and at the Burning Ghât, At the head of the flight of steps is *Dharm Kùp,* one of the sacred wells of Benares. It is situated in a small court, and is an ordinary well of which the water is none of the cleanest. In the wall surrounding the well are several small shrines occupied by images of Shiva, one of which is called Devadâseswar, and here divine honours are paid to the devout Râjâ. Near the gate of the enclosure is a stone emblem of Shiva over four feet in height. Just below Mir Ghât is a ruin called Mir Pushta after a certain Nawâb Mir Rastam Ali, who was Subadar of Benares in the time of Balwant Singh, and had his residence here.

Lalita Ghat. As his boat nears this ghât the visitor will discern, through the feathery branches of a widespreading tamarind, the gilded pinnacle of the *Nepaulese Temple,* and when the boat comes abreast of the building one of the most picturesque objects on the river bank is presented to view. The temple has a curious Chinese look about it, and is quite unique in Benares. It is surmounted by what looks like an inverted bell but is really intended for an umbrella, and all along the edges of the roof brass bells are hung, which, as moved by the breeze give forth a not unpleasing sound. The temple is sacred to Shiva and is occupied by the usual emblem of that deity, and before the door crouches a large bull carved in black stone. There is attached to the temple a Dharmsála, or pilgrim's inn, which is frequented by Hindú pilgrims from Nepál.

Rajrajeswari Ghat can hardly be called a ghát, as the flight of steps has not been added to complete it, but the façade of the building is worthy of notice as a good specimen of the mixed style of Hindú and Moresque architecture. The lower half of the middle compartment is Hindù, while the stone gallery above with the parapet and domes at the corners is Moorish. It was built by Gosáin Bhawáni Gìr.

The Burning Ghat, or Jalsain Ghat. Just below the Nepaulese Temple the bank of the river is crowned by a vast mass of lofty spires and temples which overshadow some of the most sacred spots in Benares. The first of these is the place where, under the shadow of temple spires, the pious Hindú gives his dead to the flames. The little muddy creek where this takes place is dedicated to Vishnu under the name of Jalsái, "the sleeper on the water," a name appropriate to the spot where the ashes of the pious dead are sprinkled on the bosom of "mother Ganga." The old and picturesque temple above the ghát is called Rájá Balabh ka Shiválá. The traveller as he lands will notice a number of upright stones, each decorated with rudely carved figures of a husband and wife standing hand in hand. Each of these stones marks the spot where, in olden times, some faithful wife underwent *Suttee* and was burnt alive on the same pyre as her dead husband..

It is not often that one or more cremations are not

in progress at this spot, but as the process in a somewhat lengthy one a brief description may not be out of place here. The corpse is brought to the ghât tied upon a rude bier of bamboos and carried on the shoulders of relatives, who as they move through the city streets keep up a chant of, "Râma nâma satya hai," "The name of Ram is true." The corpse, swathed in a white cloth if a male, in a red one if a female, is, at the ghât, deposited with its feet in the holy Ganges while the pyre is being prepared. Wood for the pyre may be purchased on the spot though in some cases relatives bring it with them, expensive scented woods being sometimes used by the wealthy. After the pyre has been constructed and the corpse laid thereon comes the ceremony of applying the fire. A very curious feature of this rite is the position held by the Ghât attendant. This man is always a Dom, a caste so degraded that should he, inadvertently even, touch a dead body it would be contaminated beyond remedy. And yet by an ancient rule the necessary materials for cremation must be obtained from one of this despised caste. Sherring in his "Castes and Tribes of Benares" says, "The Dom supplies five logs of wood which he lays in order on the ground, the rest of the wood being given by the family of the deceased. When the pile is ready for burning a handful of lighted straw is brought by the Dom and is taken from him and applied by one of the chief members of the family to the wood. The Dom is the only person who can furnish the light for the purpose and if from any circumstance the services of one cannot be obtained great delay and inconvenience are apt to arise. The Dom exacts a fee for three things, the five logs, the bunch of straw, and the light."

When all is ready, the son of the deceased, if he be fortunate enough to possess one, comes forward and receives in his right hand a torch. After walking with this seven times round the pyre, taking care to keep his left hand away from the pile, he sets fire to it at the head and the foot and soon all is in a blaze. The relatives withdraw to the top of the bank, where they sit in mournful silence, watching the body of the departed friend or relative being slowly reduced to ashes, and when all is consumed the ashes are gathered together and flung out on the bosom of the river.

Not unfrequently the visitor will observe some poor creature gasping out its last breath near this spot content to die near the sacred stream, and others again may be seen who have been carried here in their last agony and have passed away before arriving.

The unfinished building to the left of the ghát is the Umrao Gìr Pushtá, left in its present unfinished state on the death of the builder.

Manikarnaka Ghat. This is the most famous of all the bathing places, and it takes its name and derives its sanctity from the kund or well at the top of the steps. On the steps of this ghát, and on the long piers which jut out into the water and thus materially increase the bathing space, may be observed in all its forms and phases the ceremony of religious bathing as practised by the Hindùs. On these projecting piers sit devotees who for hours daily give themselves to the repetition of prayers and charms, and go through a great variety of ceremonies consisting of postures, bathings and libations innumerable. The ghàt is considered the central spot on the river bank and from it pilgrims set out to perform the famous *Pànch Kosi Pilgrimage.* The pilgrims travel southwards and after performing the sacred task return to the ghàt from the north dropping barley as they go, to finish at the old temple of Siddha Vinàyak, near the head of the ghàt. The massive stone ghàt, as well as the two temples at the north and south extremities, was built by the famous Maráthá princess, Ahylá Bái of Indore, a seated figure of whom in white marble adorns the front of the massive stone marhí at the south end of the ghât.

Ascending the bank the visitor comes to the famous *Manikarnikà Kund.* Within a railed enclosure is a square tank, having on each of its sides a staircase of stone leading down to a pool of stagnant water, fœtid with the rotting flowers which have been cast into it as offerings. In this the visitor sees the most sacred spot in Benares. To bathe in that filthy water means to the Hindù to obtain deliverance from all penalties, even for sins of the deepest dye. The liar, the thief, the murderer and the adulterer, may here wash and be clean, in a spot which the foot of the purest Christian man or woman would instantly defile. There are many legends connected with this well, the most common being the following: "Once upon a time the good lord Vishnu in a time of great drought dug out with his discus, not without great pain and labour, this well, to succour his faithful worshippers. His sacred sweat filled it to the brim with a pearly flood, and when Mahâdeo arrived and looked into its limpid depths he saw reflected, as in a mirror, his own charming visage. Enraptured with the sight and full of the praises of Vishnu, he asked him to name for himself some great reward, to which the dutiful Vishnu replied, that he could wish for nothing better than that he might always have the company of Mahâdeo himself. Now great indeed was the delight of the god, and in the excess of his emotion his body trembled with rapture, when lo! from one of his ears right into the midst of the well, there fell a jewelled pendant, making it sacred for all time. And this is why, to this day, it is called Manikarnikâ, the Well of the Ear-ring."

Between the well and the ghât on a raised platform is a small marble representation of two minute feet. This is the *Charana Páduká*, the monument of Vishnu's foot, for here, it is said, the god alighted and marked the spot for ever by the sign of his own footprints.

Now let the visitor look round him, for he is at the very heart of Hinduism. Above him towers a lofty temple, the gift of the Rájá of Ahmety, and below, along the edge of the sacred stream, are several others, massive and richly carved, but all slowly sinking into the bed of the mighty river. Around him surges a motley throng of pilgrims and devotees of all kind. Here is the naked yogi with matted locks and smeared from head to foot with sacred ashes, and side by side with him the gentle Sanyási, as clean as the other is foul, carrying in one hand his gourd of sacred water, and in the other his bamboo wand, which never touches the ground. Nuzzling about among the crowd, foraging for sacred flowers and leaves and dropped rice, are sacred bulls, and at your ear comes the familiar whine, "Bakhshish give here, sir; one rupee, eight annas, four annas. I am priest, sir, I make prayer for you," and turning, one sees what is surely not the least sad of all the melancholy sights here, a fine young Brahmin, with fair skin and intelligent features, over which the shadow of greed and cunning is only just creeping, taking up the mixed rôle of beggar, tout, bully aud general fraud, probably in succession to one of the fat Sons of the Ganges, squatted down there by the water side. Small comfort it is to know that his few words of broken English were learned in a Government College, or perchance in a Mission School. But saddest of all is it to see the little bands of pilgrims, whose dress proves them to be strangers to Benares, who are hurried from shrine to shrine by hired touts. Slowly they descend the steps of the sacred well, and dazed and half cowed, seat themselves in a row. Down by them squats a Brahman, twice born of heaven. His unctuous voice rolls out a few magic mantras which the poor creatures with bowed heads try to repeat, the bits of sacred grass are twisted round the fingers and stuck into the girdle, one by one the sacred ingredients, flowers, leaves, rice, &c.,

are added to the pile in their hands, and then a final dab on the shoulder of each, and out comes the fat hand, and the little eyes glitter as from crevices of the waist band, and the corner of the cloth are brought out one by one the hoarded coins. Then a step or two, and the little company ducks down into the noisome flood and all is over, the crown of piety is won.

Scindia Ghat. Just above Manikarniká Ghát is the magnificent ruin of what promised to be the most beautiful ghát on the river side. It was erected on the ruins of an old ghat sacred to Bireswar. In order to build this ghat it is said that the Maharaja Scindia in 1829 paid Rs. 15,000 to the priests to allow him, for a time only, to dispossess them though he promised to reinstate them when the ghat was finished. The steps and massive stone marhis remain intact, but the foundation of the upper portion has given way and the whole structure has fallen backwards, a wide rent being distinctly traceable along the top of the steps. The carving on the turrets is in many places imperfect, but in great part is quite finished, and the visitor may obtain some idea from it of the beautiful structure which was intended, although the life size carved figures of sepoys with musket and bayonet, which were to be inserted in the front, would hardly have adorned the structure, in the eyes of Europeans at least. Near to Scindiá Ghát may sometimes be seen immense reclining figures made of mud and coloured to represent terrific giants. They are meant to represent Bhìma and Arjuna, two of the heroes of the Mahábhárata.

Sankata Ghat is remarkable for a temple and a canopied portico which adorn the top of the steps. They were erected by a Maráthá lady, Gahná Bái, in honour of the goddess Sankatá Devi whose shrine is in the Mahallá just above the ghát. Under the portico the Shástras are read daily by Brahmins appointed for the purpose.

Ganga Mahal Ghat is so named from a shrine to Gangá, the Ganges, just behind it. The building has a peculiar shape. In the centre is a round pilaster connected with an octagonal one on each side of it by two flights of stairs, which thus traverse the front of the building. Along the top of the pilasters runs a balcony decorated with stone lattice work. At the top of the ghàt are two flaring red figures of Hanumán.

Ghonsla Ghat. This is one of the finest buildings on the banks of the river, the only one in any way equal to it in appearance being Munshi Ghát. Standing on a spot where the river makes a sharp turn, it is practically isolated from the gháts on either side of it, and its elegant proportions show to great advantage. The two massive octagonal pilasters which form the ends of the building, are connected above by an open verandha, and above that is an open gallery, the roof of which is supported on a row of elegant stone pillars. In the centre of the building is a double arched door, from which a flight of steps leads to a Vishnu Temple above. The ghát and temple were built by the Rájá of Nágpore, about one hundred years ago.

Agneswar Ghat. This is a very low, insignificant looking building. It was built by the last Peshwá of Poona, Báji Ráo. The small stone canopies which crown the two ends are connected by a beautiful creeping plant which gives it a very picturesque appearance.

Ram Ghat. This is a heavy looking stone building, coloured a dull orange and containing a large collection of brass images of Rám and his companions. It is an ancient ghát having been built over two hundred years ago by the Rájá of Jaipur.

Lakshman Bala Ghat is situated where the river takes an abrupt curve inward, towards the lofty bank crowned by the Minarets. The imposing building with its long rows of black window frames and venetian shutters was erected by Báji Ráo, the last of the Maráthá

Peshwás, and the predecessor of the infamous Náná Sahib. It is now owned by the Mahárájá of Scindia. The round stone building in front is a temple to Raghuveswar.

Panch Ganga Ghat. This is one of the five most sacred ghàts on the river, and receives its name from the fact, as Hindús believe, that at this spot four other rivers join the Ganges. These four streams are, Dharma Nada, (river of virtue) Dhútapápá, (cleanser of sin) Kirnanadí, (brook of sun rays) and the Saraswatí, (spouse of Brahma). This is a most sacred spot, where even the gods find merit in bathing. The ghát abounds in shrines which are in many cases occupied by not one, but several idols. The large stone erection at the corner of the ghát, resembling an open pine cone, is a lamp stand, used on festive occasions when the ghát is illuminated. It is said to be capable of holding a thousand lamps. The ghát is said to have been built by Rájá Mán Singh, three hundred years ago.

Madho Rai Ghat is really a part of Pánch Gangá Ghát, and it leads up to an old door-way from which the visitor may obtain a most picturesque view of the ghát and river below.

Durga Ghat is closely united with the preceding ghát. It is named from a temple to Dúrgá, the black faced, blood-thirsty spouse of Shiva, which is situated at the top of the steps.

Brahma Ghat. This is an ancient ghát of irregular form but very picturesque in appearance, with its winding steps and overhanging trees. Next to the Mán Mandir it is probably the oldest building on the bank of the river. It is much frequented by Maráthá ladies, and was repaired by the Peshwá Báji Ráo some sixty years ago.

Rajmandir Ghat is a long bathing place crowned by a stone embankment or pushta. Above may be seen the back wall of a lofty building, formerly the residence of a Rájá, after whom the ghát is named.

Sitala Ghat is so named from a temple sacred to Sítalá, the goddess of small-pox, which is on the southern side of the ghát. The temple has a peculiar appearance, being painted red on the lower part and whitewashed above. It is not much frequented, the more popular shrine of this goddess being situated at Dasaswamedh Ghát.

Gal Ghat stands out on a little promontory. It is remarkable for its square stone pilasters. Below this ghát is a long stretch of bank, bare of interest, until we come to

Trilochan Ghat. This is a famous ghát, and takes its name from the ancient shrine above it. Trílochan means three-eyed, and is an epithet of Shivá who rejoices in a third eye situated in the middle of his forehead. There are two low turrets at the foot of this ghát between which the pilgrim must bathe, as the water on either side has no special sanctity.

Prahlad Ghat is the last of the ghâts towards the north. It is one of the most picturesque of all the ghâts, whether viewed from the river or regarded from the bank. It stands on a sharp bluff jutting out into the stream, and from it may be obtained a splendid view of the whole river bank as it extends southwards in a noble curve. The top of the ghât is delightfully shaded by several large trees, and forms a lounging place very much appreciated by the natives of this part. *Barnà Sangam Ghàt* is below the Dufferin Bridge, and distant nearly three quarters of a mile from Prahlád Ghát. It is best reached by land.

GOLDEN TEMPLE, OR TEMPLE OF VISWESWAR NATH. This is by far the most important temple in Benares, and may be regarded as the very centre of Shiva worship in the city. The building is enclosed in a court-yard surrounded by a covered verandha, and is capped by two spires and a central dome. The dome and one of the spires are covered with copper plates, heavily gilded, the gift of Ranjít Singh, the famous Sikh Prince and once the proud possessor of the Koh-i-núr. The deity in this temple, which is placed under the gilded spire, is the usual Shiva emblem, and the attention of the god is called to the devotions of its worshippers by as many as nine bells, some of them of considerable beauty, which hang suspended under the gilded dome. Over the outer door-way of the temple is a brass figure of Ganesh, and on one side a representation of the Sun and on the other of the Moon. Worshippers as they enter, dash a few spots of Ganges water or a few flowers up at this figure to ensure the favour of the eldest son and chief counsellor of Shiva. By ascending to an upper room in a flower vendor's shop opposite the door of the temple, the visitor may obtain a clear view of the gilded roofs, and of the crowd of worshippers in the lane below. At no other spot in Benares, save perhaps at the Manikarniká Ghát can such evidence be observed of the vitality of idolatry. This pushing, jostling, earnest crowd of men and women with their hands full of suitable gifts, are bent on one thing only, and that is to prostrate themselves before, and to present their offerings to, a conical black stone, capable of suggesting nothing at all in itself, and bearing only an imposed meaning of the most degrading kind.

Behind the temple is an immense collection of idols, called the Kachahri or court-house of Shiva. It is probable that some of them were placed here when Jehangir destroyed the great temple of Visweswar near by.

The visitor should next proceed either to the Gyán Bápi or the Anna Purná Temple.

GYAN BAPI OR WELL OF KNOWLEDGE. This is a famous well close to the Golden Temple, the water of which is said to bestow the knowledge of salvation. The well is said to derive its miraculous powers from an emblem of Shiva which originally graced the ancient Temple of Visweswar near by. When that fine structure was destroyed by the Emperor Jehangir the deity, though only a conical stone, voluntarily cast itself into this well, where, in the belief of the faithful, it still resides. The well is surrounded by a stone screen breast high, and as devotees are constantly casting into it flowers and fruits as offerings to the deity, the authorities have prudently covered the mouth of the well with sheets of iron to prevent the fouling of the water. By the side of the well sits an attendant who ladles out to the worshiphers the sacred water, and in return receives their offerings. The well is covered by a fine canopy of stone supported by forty pillars. The canopy was erected by a Maráthá princess, Sri Maut Baijá Bái of Gwalior, in 1828. Near the well is an immense Nandi or Bull of Shiva. It is a monolith, seven feet in heght, the gift of the Rájá of Nepál. Close to it is a small shrine, somewhat elevated, containing an image of Shiva. Images of this deity are uncommon, as he is usually sufficiently represented by the lingam, but in this case we have him completely depicted, with his terrible third eye in the centre of his forehead and around his neck a garland of skulls. Seated on his left knee is Párbati, his wife, who holds in her lap the infant Ganesh. Near by is the Gyán Bapi Mosque.

GYAN BAPI MOSQUE, so called because of its proximity to the Gyán Bápi or Well of Knowledge. It is the principal mosque in the city and is remarkable from having been constructed by the Emperor Jehangir, son of Akbar the Great, out of the ruins of a magnificent temple of Visweswar, a portion of which may still be seen at the back of the Mosque. The Mosque itself is not without some claims to beauty, but it is impossible to obtain a good view of the front of it by reason of the fact that the chief entrance has been closed, as the result of a fierce conflict between the Muhammadans and the Hindús as to the right of way over the courtyard outside. The Hindùs prevailed and the Mosque enclosure is entered from the side. Here the visitor may observe the large numer of beautiful carved stone columns which support the front of the Mosque and which formerly adorned the old Temple. The aspect of this Mosque, in its cleanliness and quiet, affords a striking contrast to the noisy and noisome courts of idolatry close by.

Proceeding to the back of the mosque the visitor may obtain some idea of the magnificence of the former temple. Judging from the portion now remaining it must have been much larger than any temple now existing in Benares. Antiquarians see in these ruins a mixture of Jain and Hindú styles of architecture, and indeed it is thought that the Hindú Temple was preceded by a Buddhist Víhára or Monastery. What appear to be cloisters of this Monastery, may be observed under the terrace of the Mosque, just opposite the stone bull near the Well of Knowledge. The cloister consists of small chambers, the roof of which is supported by square pillars of a primitive type of architecture said by experts to be Buddhistic. The cloister is blackened with smoke, being used as a cooking room by the Hindú attendants at the well.

In the "Autobiography of Jehangir" the Emperor gives the following account of the destruction of the ancient temple of Visweswar. "I am here led to relate that at the city of Benares a temple had been created by Rájá Mán Singh, which had cost him 36 lakhs of ashrafis. The principal idol in the temple had on its head a tiara or cap enriched with jewels to the value of three lakhs of ashrafis. He had placed in this temple morever, as the associates and ministering servants of the principal idol, four other images of solid gold each crowned with a tiara in like manner enriched with precious stones. It was the belief of these Jahannamites that a dead Hindù, provided when alive he had been a worshipper, when laid before this idol would be restored to life. As I could not possibly give credit to such a pretence,

I employed a confidential person to ascertain the truth, and as I justly supposed the whole was detected to be an impudent imposture. Of this discovery I availed myself and made it my plan for throwing down the temple which was the scene of this imposture, and on the spot with the very same materials I erected the great mosque, because the very name of Islam was proscribed at Benares, and with God's blessing it is my desire, if I live, to fill it full of true believers."

JAIN TEMPLE. The most accessible of the ten or twelve temples belonging to the sect of Jains in Benares is situated in a garden near the front of the Town Hall. The Jains, though they were never Buddhists, still preserve in India some of the distinctive Buddhist doctrines. They reject the Vedas except so far as they confirm their own doctrines, and are free from the extravagant idolatry which marks Hinduism. They hold in supreme reverence certain saintly souls, who by meditation are believed to have raised themselves to the highest spiritual altitude. Of these they reckon twenty four in the present era, and images of them hold places of honour in their temples. In the temple here described a large number of such images will be observed placed on an altar in the inner shrine. The twenty-third of these Jains, or spiritual heroes, was Párasnáth, whose image is occasionally found alone in their temples. The last was Mahábír, now regarded as a historical personage contemporary with Buddha. The Jains are a small, but wealthy sect, and their temples are sometimes very beautiful, and always scrupulously clean, being in this point most agreeable contrasts to the Shiválas of the Hindús. They have the most scrupulous regard for animal and vegetable life in every form, and the more punctilious dust their seats carefully before occupying them, and wear a piece of fine linen over their mouths when drinking water to prevent the untimely death of any insect.

KAMESHWAR TEMPLE. This temple is situated in a lane to the south of Machaudari Tank, and is sacred to Shiva as the Lord of Desire. It is an old shrine, and but little used except on festive occasions and by pilgrims. At the right hand of the entrance is a small temple with a collection of idols, and within, in the first courtyard, is a large kettle-drum. The second or inner courtyard is literally crowded with temples and stone figures of deities. The largest temple is sacred to Kámeshwar, the image inside being the usual linga set in a brass cistern. Around the base of a large peepul tree which overshadows the court, is a collection of stone deities of various kinds, one being of the goddess Machaudari riding on a peacock, and another of the Sun. In a wall of the verandah near by is a carved image of Narsingh, the Man-lion incarnation of Vishnu. He is a horrible monster with a lion face, and has on his knees a victim whom he is disembowelling with his claws. Opposite this revolting representation of the divine is a bas-relief of a saint, the Rishi Durvás, who by his asceticism is said to have attained equality with Vishnu. In the next verandah are images of Rám and Sitá, and on every hand is a great profusion of idols of all sorts.

LAT BHAIRO. On the left hand side of the road as the traveller goes to Ráj Ghát, and near the junction with it of the old Ghazipur road, is a tank, and above it a paved plateau, the whole of which, with the exception of a small square enclosure, is now a Muhammadan Mosque. This Mosque was rebuilt about sixty years ago by Mirza Buláki, one of the exiled princes of the old Mogul family who live in Benares. In the little enclosure referred to is a pillar smothered with red pigment, which is regarded by Hindús with great reverence. It is called the Lát, or club, of Bhairo. It once stood within the enclosure of a temple which was destroyed by order of Aurangzeb, and the stones used to build the outer wall of the place of prayer. The present pillar is only a fragment of the original one which was thrown down and broken in a struggle between the Hindús and Muhammadans in 1805 The tank below the platform is the Kapilmochan Tank.

LOLARIK KUAN. This remarkable well is just behind the engine house of the pumping station at Bhadaini. The massive stone-work of the well is the work of three persons, Ráni Ahalya Bái, a Rájá of Behar, and Amrit Rao. The well proper is a round shaft, about fifteen feet in diameter and protected by a strong breastwork of masonry of great thickness. The water below flows through a lofty archway into a stone reservoir in the shape of a parallelogram, which is reached from above by three massive and steep flights of stone-steps. The whole presents an appearance of great solidity and strength, and the lofty arch connecting the round shaft with the square opening, has such an air of grace and lightness, as serves to place this well among the most interesting sights of its kind in Benares. The motive for the peculiar construction of the well is not apparent, but the connection of the round shaft with the parallelogram below distinctly suggests the form of the linga, the common emblem of Shiva. On the steps of the well is a most absurd figure of Ganesh in which that deity is depicted in an erect attitude. In the walls of the well are several carved stones, evidently of a great age, and probably brought here from some old shrine.

MINARETS, THE, or MOSQUE of AURANGZEB. This Mosque is called by natives of Benares, Mádho Dás ká Dharahrá, or the Minárs of Mádho Dás, that being the name of the Hindú builder who, at the command of the Emperor, erected these beautiful structures. The Mosque to which they are attached is at the top of Pánch Gangá Ghát, and forms the most commanding, and certainly the most beautiful feature of the long array of edifices which line the river bank. The Mosque itself is said to have been erected from the materials of an immense temple to Vishnu which once stretched along the river bank, and the Minarets were erected to annoy Hindús by making it possible to overlook the interiors of their dwellings. There can be no question of the beauty and extreme gracefulness of these lofty towers. A recent French traveller, M. André Chevrillon, says of them, "They spring straight upwards, with the ardor of a prayer, with the impetuosity of a cry; and one perceives the fervent work of a simple, resolute, monotheistic and ardent race."

Seated in the little cage at the top, the whole of the city lies at one's feet and one seems, like the pigeons which circle beneath, to be poised in mid air. The ascent, though difficult, is by no means dangerous and the view from the summit more than repays the labour. The height from the base of the Mosque to the top of the minarets is 142 feet. The minarets are 8¼ feet in diameter at the base, 7½ at the summit. The Mussulmán attendant is entitled to a small fee.

Descending from the Mosque the visitor will observe a peepul tree, round the base of which is a perfect pantheon of Hindù deities. Here too is an old door-way, opening on to the ghát, from which may be obtained a most picturesque view of the ghát, the river, and the Dufferin Bridge beyond.

From this point the visitor may make his way through winding streets, truly oriental in character, to the Brass Bazaar and thence to the Chauk, a most interesting walk.

MISSIONARY SOCIETIES IN BENARES. Visitors to Benares who are interested in the present relations of Christianity to Hinduism, will hardly fail to pay a visit to one or other of the Christian missions here represented. Missionaries are always ready to shew their schools &c. to persons interested in their work, and ladies specially may in this way obtain an insight into the domestic life of Indian women which would otherwise be difficult or impossible. Tourists might well devote the

Sunday, so usually spent in "doing" this or that portion of the city, to a sympathetic enquiry into the present state of missions, and to obtaining a view at first hand of the labours of the men and women who here hold up the standard of Christ. English services are held in three churches on the Sunday, and Hindustani services at several others, to all of which visitors are cordially welcomed. A few words on each of the Societies here represented may not be out of place.

Baptist Missionary Society. This was a branch of the Serampur Mission established here in 1819, and this Society had the honour of sending the first English Missionary to Benares. In 1890 the male missionary was withdrawn, but work is still carried on among women and girls in connection with the Baptist Zenána Mission.

Church Missionary Society. This Society has its head quarters at Sigra, where there is a church, a normal school for girls, a girls' orphanage, and Christian village. The mission has charge also of a very large school situated in the Bengali Tola, called Jay Narayan's College, after the enlightened native gentleman who built and endowed it, and who, acting on the advice of the devoted Corrie, a former chaplain in Benares, handed it over to the Church Mission in 1817. The Society has also a church in the centre of the city which the visitor cannot fail to notice, and in which services are held which are attended at times by large numbers of intelligent Hindùs. Services in Hindustani are held in the Sigra Church morning and afternoon.

London Missionary Society. This Society has its head quarters near the Cantonments Station where the houses of the Missionaries are situated, together with the church and girls' school. The work of the Society is educational and evangelistic, and in connection with it there is a number of girls' school in different parts of the city, and a large amount of Zenána visitation is done. There is a High School connected with the Mission and also a boarding house for christian boys. The Society commenced work in Benares in 1820. An English service is held in the church at 11 A. M. during the cold season, and Hindustani services at 8–30 A. M. and 4 P. M.

Wesleyan Missionary Society. This Society commenced work in Benares in 1880. The Mission has a fine church in a prominent situation near the Post Office, in which services are held in English at 11 A. M. and 6 P. M., and in Hindustani at 8 A. M. The resident Missionary is Chaplain to the Wesleyan soldiers in the garrison, and also superintends the work of several catechists. There is also Zenána and Girls' School work carried on in connection with the Mission.

Zenana Bible and Medical Mission. This Society has two centres of work. One is at Rámkatorá, near the Queen's College, where the ladies reside who have charge of the Girls' School and Zenána work. There is also a very handsome Hospital for women connected with this Society, situated in the Aurangabad road near Sigra. The Hospital was opened in 1890, and there are connected with it several branch dispensaries in the city.

The Missionaries in Benares meet weekly for a united Bible reading, on Thursday evenings at 8 o'clock. It is held in the houses of the Missionaries in rotation, and visitors to the city desirous of Christian communion are heartily welcomed to these meetings.

MONKEY TEMPLE, THE. This is a temple sacred to Durgá or Káli, the wife of Mahádeva. The temple has no necessary connection with the monkeys which swarm hereabouts, and it is known popularly by its connection with the kund or tank adjoining. But the monkeys are clearly in possession, and from their homes in the neighbouring tamarinds invade every part of the shrine. They scramble over the roofs, and drop down chattering and screaming, upon the verandah to seize the parched grain with which they are liberally fed by worshippers. They swarm throughout this entire neighbourhood, and will be found also at the Kurukshetr Tank and the Lolárik Well, both of which are not far away. It is related that a few years ago they existed in such large numbers, and did such damage to the roofs of the buildings hereabout that a certain magistrate, at the request of the inhabitants, caught and transported very many of them beyond the Ganges. The temple and tank are the gift of a pious Bengali lady, the Ráni Bhawáni, and are not very old. The temple is situated in a large quadrangle, the main entrance being on the west side. In front and close to the road is a Naubat Khána or band-stand, for the accommodation of musicians on special occasions. Between this and the door is a tall pillar with a figure of a lion, the proper vehicle of Durgá, on the top. Near by is a small stone pillar with a little hollow in the summit. This is the altar of the deity, and near it is a cleft post to which the animal to be sacrificed is bound. This is usually a goat. It is tied to the post by the head and an attendant lifts it up by its hind legs and holds it so that its neck is extended. With one swift blow of the heavy knife its head is severed and is immediately placed on the altar. This becomes the perquisite of the priest, while the body is taken away and consumed by the worshipper. It is openly averred that many Hindus who otherwise would never taste flesh, adopt this expedient to get a savoury meal of kid pillao. On each side of the doorway of the temple is a small shrine. Inside the main doorway are two stone lines, one on each hand, with their faces directed towards the Goddess. All round the four sides of the quadrangle is a covered verandah used by pilgrims and devotees. In front of the temple proper is a porch which was erected by a native military officer about thirty years ago. From the centre of this porch hangs a large bell which is said to have been presented by a European Magistrate of Mirzapur. The temple and porch are beautifully carved, and the floor of the porch is paved with alternate square slabs of black and white marble. Through the door of the temple may be seen the image of the Goddess, a woman with a silver face and an enormously distended red tongue, and decorated with numerous garlands of flowers. This is the deity, a thing to shudder at, which is the chosen object of worship of the mild and intelligent Bengalis who live in such lage numbers in Benares, and on Tuesday mornings her courts are thronged with worshippers, and numberless goats are slaughtered in her honor. She is the only deity who is worshipped with sacrifices of blood, and she was formerly the patroness of the bands of blood-thirsty Thugs who of old infested the roads in India. Well has she been described as,

"Dark Goddess of the azure flood,
"Whose robes are wet with infant tears;
"Skull-chaplet wearer, whom the blood
"Of men delights three thousand years."

The story of the Goddess is interesting. Originally a great demon monster, called Durg, acquired power over gods and men and ruled them with great tyranny and oppression. When appealed to for deliverance Mahádeva ordered his wife, Gauri, to slay the demon. She, taking upon herself a terrible form, waged war upon him, and after a fierce struggle in which mountains were torn from their roots and seas filled up, she overcame and slew the demon and his army. Intoxicated with delight she began to dance about among the slain with the bleeding head of Durg in her hand, and so wild were her antics that the pillars of the earth trembled. Gods and men again appealed to Mahádeva to save them from ruin and to stop the goddess in her wild frenzy, but she could not hear his voice in the madness of her joy. At last he lay down among the dead, and only when she found herself trampling on the body of her husband did the goddess, thrusting out her tongue in shame and dismay, cease from her mad career, and the earth had peace. From that time she has been named from the demon she slew, Durgá and is represented with four hands, three of which carry weapons and the fourth a bleeding head, supposed to be that of her great enemy, while she has round her neck a garland of skulls.

Near by is the Lolárik Kuán.

NAG KUAN or the SERPENT'S WELL. This in an old well situated in the Nág Kuán Mahalla in the north-western part of the city. The well is probably of great age, but the massive steps which lead down to it are not more than a hundred and fifty years old. The stairs are in the form of a square, and they lead down to a circular well at the bottom, which has on its inner wall a winding staircase of stone slabs which leads to the surface of the water. At the head of one of the staircases is an image of two snakes intertwined, and in several recesses in walls are images of the same kind. The well is visited on two days in the year in the rainy season by great crowds of people. On the first day the women, and in the second day the men, bathe in great numbers in the filthy water of the well, and make offerings to the various serpent images here to be found.

OBSERVATORY, THE MANMANDIR. This interesting building is reached by a lane which leads from the head of the Dasaswamedh Ghát. The visitor enters by a door over which is a figure of Ganesh, and traversing a winding passage he enters a courtyard open to the sky, but shaded by several trees. This courtyard is surrounded by several rooms which are occasionally occupied by pilgrims and other travellers. In the right hand corner of the courtyard is a stone staircase which leads to the roof, where are to be found the astronomical instruments for which the building is famous. These instruments were constructed by Rájá Jay Singh of Jaipur (a successor of Rájá Mán Singh who erected the main building and the ghát below) in the reign of the Emperor Muhammad Shah, 1719–1748. Jay Singh was famous for his skill in astronomy, and was appointed by the Emperor to reform the astronomical tables then in existence which were known to be inaccurate. To enable him to do this, Jay Singh erected observatories at Delhi, Mathura, Ujjain, Jaipur and Benares. The instruments in this observatory have been fully described by Pandit Bápu Deva Shástri, C. I. E., a copy of whose booklet may be obtained from the caretaker. A brief description only is here attempted. At the head of the stairs on the right hand of the visitor is a wall, on the plastered surface of which are traced two quadrants, intersecting each other and marked off into degrees. This in the *Bhattiyantra*, or mural quadrant, and was used to observe the sun's altitude and greatest declination, by which means the latitude and longitude of the place was determined. To the north of this wall is an immense instrument called the *Yantra Samrát* (prince of instruments). It consists of a central wall, called a gnomon, pointing due north, with two arcs branching form it, east and west, built of stone and marked along their edges in degrees. In the edges of the gnomon four iron rings will be observed. These are the centres of the arcs on each side. The whole instrument forms an immense sun-dial. On one of the side walls of the gnomon a mural quadrant is traced, similar to the one already described, and near by is another sun-dial of a much smaller size. Near the smaller dial is an instrument called the *Equinoctial Circle*, a larger dial with a central spike pointing directly north. By this the distance from the meridian of the sun or a star is obtained when it is in the northern hemisphere. Close to this is the *Chakra Yantra*, or wheel instrument, consisting of a circle of iron enfaced with brass, moving on an axis which points due north. There was originally an index finger of brass attached to the centre of this wheel, but it has been torn off. The instrument was used to obtain the declination of a planet or star. Near by is the largest of all the instrument, called the *Diganśá Yantra.* It consists of a central pillar 4 feet 2 inches in height, surrounded by two concentric walls, the inner one being of the same height as the pillar, and the outer exactly twice its height. Both walls are marked on their upper surfaces in degree spaces, and on the upper walls four spikes are placed to mark the cardinal points. The instrument was constructed to find the degrees of azimuth of a planet or star.

After inspecting the instruments the visitor should ascend to the roof of the building which overlooks the river, from which a splendid view of the city and the surrounding country may be obtained. Following the course of the river to the north-east, the eye is arrested by the Dufferin Bridge over the Ganges, which presents from this point a most graceful appearance. Between it and the observer is the long curved line of ghats and temples which line the left bank of the river, above which tower in stately, yet simple grandeur the minarets of the mosque of Aurangzeb. In the opposite direction the eye follows the line of ghats, and opposite the last one, on a spur of land jutting out into the river, may be observed Ramnagar, the seat of the Maharaja of Benares, while beyond it, in the horizon is seen the blue shadow of a distant line of hills. These are the northern spurs of the great Vindhya chain of mountains which run down in a south-westerly direction and join the Western Ghauts. Descending, the visitor is shown a large room overlooking the river and decorated in a somewhat gaudy style with plaster ornamentation. It is occasionally used as a conference chamber by pandits.

PANCH KOSI ROAD and PILGRIMAGE. The Panch Kosi, or ten mile road, is the boundary which marks off the sacred city from the common soil which surrounds it. All who die within this limit, of whatever creed or character, are certain of bliss in the next world. The road is a very old one though hardly so ancient as is supposed. On the Benares side of it there are numerous small shrines, the deities of which are supposed to act the part of watchmen and guardians of the sacred city. Starting from Manikarnika Kund the pilgrims proceed barefoot along the bank of the river to Assi Sangam, from which point the road branches off into the country. The first halt is at Kandhwa at a distance of about six miles from Manikarnika. Here there is a temple of considerable age and of some beauty where the Pilgrim spends the night. The next stage is to Dhupchandi, about ten miles, after which is a tramp of fourteen miles to Rameswar. From this point to Shivpur is eight miles, and here he must visit the temple of the Panch pandavàs, or the five brothers, Yudhishthira, Bhima, Arjuna, Nakula, Sahadeva, all of whom were married to one wife. From Shivpur to Kapildhara, a picturesque tank just beyond the Barna, is six miles. From this spot back to Manikarnika Ghat the pilgrim scatters on the ground grains of barley, a little of which he preserves as an offering to Yava Binayak, or the Barley Ganesh, near Manikarnika. After a visit to the temple of Sakhi Binayak near the Cow Temple, to have the performance of his task duly attested, the pilgrim may return home assured of having achieved full salvation. The road is very picturesque being lined nearly throughout by a double row of trees, the huge trunks of some of which bear witness to their great age. There are other halting places besides those mentioned at some of which very large tanks of water are situated, and it is a most picturesque sight to observe bands of pilgrims of all ages and both sexes, often singing as they go, clad in bright coloured garments passing along the road under these great trees, whose wide spreading branches cast a shade very pleasant to the travellers in the hot season of the year.

PISACH MOCHAN TANK. This tank is situated just behind the large palace of the Mahárája of Hathwa which adjoins the Chetganj Road. Pisách means demon, and Mochan, release, and the story of this tank is as follows :—" A certain powerful demon once entered Benares, and having overpowered the guardian deities who stand on guard along the Panch Kosi road, he was met at this spot by Bhaironáth, the deified Kotwál of the city. A terrific conflict ensued, in which eventually the demon was vanquished and beheaded. The head, carried before Mahádeo for judgment, pleaded its own cause to such purpose that it was decreed that not only should the demon be allowed to reside on the spot where the battle took place, but that no pilgrim should be allowed to proceed to Gaya without first bathing in this tank. In return he promised to protect the city and all who bathed in his tank from the attacks of evil spirits." The tank is greatly frequented by residents of Benares, for the belief in evil spirits is very prevalent. It is a fine sheet of water and its banks bear the ruins of several centuries. The ghát on the south side, which has almost disappeared, is said to have been constructed as long as three hundred years ago. The ghát and wall on the west were built partly by a Hindu, Balwant Ráo, and partly by a Mussalmán, Mirza Khurram Sháh, about a hundred years ago. The north ghát on which are the ruins of several stone structures, was the work of a Hindu, Rájá Murlidhar, about a hundred and twenty years since. On the east side are the temples and the abodes of the Brahmin priests. The chief temple is an old structure, really consisting of a group of shrines, out of the centre of which spring two sacred trees, a peepul and a banyan intertwined. Under the shade of these trees may be seen the great head of the demon Pisach, a grinning monster fearful to behold; next to him is a four-handed Vishnu, and near by a large figure of Hanumán. Here is also a peculiar figure of Ganesh with five trunks, three straight and two curled. There is also a large number of other idols, mostly emblems of Shiva.

QUEEN'S COLLEGE. This beautiful building is situated near the Jagat Ganj road and is well worth a visit. It is claimed for it that it is one of the finest buildings erected by the British in Northern India. It was designed by, and erected under the superintendence of Major Kittoe, R. E., the famous archaeologist. It is faced with Chunar stone, and the various small towers and arcades are embellished with inscriptions in the Nágari character and in English, recording the names of the persons at whose expense the various portions were erected. In addition to the very large sums thus subscribed, the building cost the government £12,690. The grounds are beautifully laid out and contain, near the Principal's residence, a great collection of carved stones, mostly Buddhistic, brought here from Sárnath and other places. There is also a large pillar, a monolith 32 feet in height, which was found on the banks of the Ganges near Ghazipur. It was erected here in 1854 at the expense of the Hon. James Thomason, Lieut. Governor of these Provinces. It has an inscription in the Gupta character and so may be said to date from the fourth century of our era.

As an educational Institution, the character of the College is deservedly high. It is affiliated with the Allahabad University, and prepares students for the examinations of that body. It also gives instruction in law, and there is an important Sanscrit department. Connected with the College is a High School, which teaches from the lowest standard up to the Entrance Examination of the University. The school has a large Boarding-house connected with it. School and College combined give instruction to over 700 students.

RAJ GHAT PLATEAU. From the Kashi Railway Station, along the bank of the Ganges to its junction with the Barná, stretches a triangular shaped tongue of land, on which, tradition says, was once situated the massive fort of Rájá Banár. There is no historical evidence to prove this old time tale, but this lofty plateau, commanding the city, above which it towers some thirty-five feet, and defended on two of its sides by the Barná, and the Ganges, was undoubtedly at one time occupied by masses of buildings and was the seat of a considerable population. At the time of the Mutiny it was fortified by the British, but was deserted in 1865 on account of its unhealthiness. The only object of interest now visible is the tomb of Lál Muhammad Khán, a soldier of fortune. The inscription over the entrance to the tomb bears a date corresponding to 1768 A. D.

RAM NAGAR FORT. This is the seat of the Mahárájá of Benares, and is situated on the right bank of the Ganges, about a mile above Assi Ghát. To reach it, the traveller must drive past Durgá Kund to Kamachha Ghát, a distance of about four miles from Cantonments. From thence he will be able to obtain a boat across to the Fort.

Before visiting the Fort, and to enable the visitor to inspect the interior of the palace, and the Rájá's Garden House, a permit should be obtained from the Mahárájá's private secretary who resides at Rámnagar. The appearance of the fort on approaching it from the river is striking, the round buttresses giving it an air of great solidity. The interior of the palace will not impress the visitor accustomed to the greater splendours of Europe, but the view of the city from the balcony overlooking the river is superb. There is also here to be seen a temple dedicated to Vedavyás, the compiler of the Vedas. About a mile from Rámnagar Fort is a famous tank, and a very beautiful temple, both well worthy of a visit, and as they are both contiguous to a very pleasant garden and garden-house, they form a suitable place for an afternoon picnic. The tank is a very fine one and was constructed by Rájá Cheit Singh, and has been rendered peculiarly sacred by its associations with Vedavyás. Usually, to die on the right bank of the Ganges involves transmigration into the body of an ass, but whoever, at the special festival in which Vedavyás is honoured, bathes in this tank is sure to escape that terrible transformation. The temple near the tank is one of the most beautiful and certainly the most elaborate in these parts. It was begun by Cheit Singh and completed by his successors. It is litearally covered with scores, nay hundreds of sculptured figures, in which sacred animals, incarnations, saints and deities are represented in great profusion, all being most carefully carved. The temple is thus a splendid specimen of modern Hindu sculpture.

ST. MARY'S CHURCH. This is the station church, and is in charge of the Chaplain. It is pleasantly situated in a large enclosure opposite Clark's Hotel, and is capable of seating four or five hundred persons. There are no monuments of any interest in the building nor can it lay claim to any architectural beauty. The spire, which was added in 1827, transformed what was a plain unpretentious structure into an architectural enormity The following inscriptions are to be found on the base of the font.

"This church was first erected by subscription under the direction and personal superintendence of James Robinson, Esq., A. D. 1815."

"The first stone of this church was laid by the Rev. Daniel Corrie, Chaplain."

"This church was consecrated by the Right Reverend Father in God, Reginald Heber, Lord Bishop of Calcutta, 5th September, 1824."

"This church was enlarged and repaired at the expense of Government, and the steeple, pulpit, and organ loft, were erected by private subscription under the superintendence of James Prinsep in 1827–28. The clock was presented by Babu Shiv Narayan Singh, 1829."

Services are held at 11 A. M. and 6 P. M. during the cold season.

SAKHI BINAYAK TEMPLE. In a lane just behind the Anna Púrná Temple is the temple of the deity who is supposed to verify the fact that pilgrims have faithfully performed the Pánch Kosi pilgrimage. The presiding deity is Ganesh, a great red image of whom faces the door. Unless the fact of the performance be registered here, the poor pilgrim can have no hope of profiting by the merit he has so laboriously acquired.

SANICHAR or SATURN. An image of this deity may be seen near the door of the Golden Temple. The image has a silver face from which an apron depends which conceals the fact that the deity is bodiless.

SARNATH. This is the site of the famous Buddhistic remains, and is situated a little to the left of the trunk road from Benares to Ghazipur, at about three miles distance from Benares. The name is applied locally to a small temple to Shiva, not far distant from the ruins, and is supposed to be an appellation of that many-named deity. By others it is said to be equivalent to Sálá Náth, Sálá meaning brother-in-law, and the legend is that a brother-in-law of Shiva when on a visit to his relative, was induced to take up his permanent abode here. The usual meaning among the learned is declared to be Sáranganáth, lord of the deer, in which case the name is a relic of ancient times, when all this region was a vast deer park, in which Buddha in one of his incarnations ranged as lord of a herd.

The remains now in existence consist of two large ruined towers, and a vast mass of broken bricks, evidently the ruins of former monasteries, chapels and temples. The larger tower is called the *Dhamek*, and is an immense solid mass of brick and stone, rising 128 feet above the general level of the country. The lower part of the tower, to a height of 43 feet, is built entirely of Chunar stone, and in the erection no mortar was used, but each stone, even in the very centre of the mass, is clamped to its fellows by iron bands. The upper mass, consisting of large bricks, was probably originally plastered over and surmounted by a pinnacle bearing a gilt umbrella. In 1835 a shaft was sunk with great labour down the centre of the tower to the foundations, but nothing of great importance was discovered, and it is generally supposed that the tower was erected to be a lasting memorial of the Buddhistic creed. The carving on the stone portion of the tower is very beautiful and is in places well preserved. Around the tower there are eight projecting faces in the centre of each of which is a niche 5½ feet high in which pedestals still remain which probably each carried a figure of Buddha. Seven of these eight faces are richly carved around the niches, the carving in places being evidently unfinished. Around the building runs a triple band of ornamentation. The middle and broadest band consists of various geometrical figures, cut with great precision and clearness. The upper band consists of a scroll ornament of the lotus plant, with leaves and buds only, while in the lower band the lotus is represented in full bloom. The exact age of the tower it is impossible precisely to determine, as no inscription or record establishing the fact has been discovered, but its form is said to belong to the seventh century of our era. The extensive mass of ruined brick surrounding the tower will give the visitor some faint idea of the great buildings that once existed here. Vast quantities of materials, both stone and brick, have been removed at various times to the city to be used for building purposes, and the only remnant of the scores of statues, bas reliefs, &c., which once existed here, are two mutilated images imbedded in the earth, the one to the south-east and the other to the northwest of the Dhamek.

As a result of the excavations made by Cunningham in 1834–35 and Kittoe in 1851, the foundations of very extensive buildings were discovered consisting of monasteries and temples and also the remains of a very ancient stupa, or tower, the hemispherical shape of which shewed it to belong to the earliest style of Buddhist architecture. An inscription was brought to light which showed that this ancient tower had been repaired in 1026 A. D. and at the same time a large number of statues and bas reliefs, exquisitely carved, were rescued from the ruins and transferred, some to the grounds of the Queen's College, and some to the Museum at Calcutta, where they may still be seen. Evdience was also discovered of the fury with which at last Brahminism extinguished the religion of Buddha. The charred beams, with nails still transfixed, showed that fire had completed the devastation, and how sudden and remorseless the attack had been, was shewn by the quantities of food found prepared but yet uncooked, and nodules of brass from vessels melted in the flames, while heaps of blackened bones gave evidence that all the inhabitants had not time to escape.

Now let the traveller pause and glance around. He stands, as it were, on the water-shed of two great religious systems. Here parted for ever, Brahminism and Buddhism, for with the destruction of Sarnath the milder faith passed to a greater empire and a wider sway in the farther east, where now the teeming millions of Burma, Japan and China own her rule. To us both religions are mighty, mysterious and awe-inspiring. Between them they rule the destinies of more than half the human race and both sprang to life and grew to vigorous power near where we are standing, amid these shattered bricks, under the shadow of this ruined tower!

Near the Dhamek is a Jain temple which the attendant priest will exhibit to visitors. It contains an image in black marble of Párasnáth, the last but one of the Jain divinities. About half of a mile to the south of the Dhamek is the second towar called the *Chaukandi*. It is octagonal in form, 23 feet in height, and raised on a mound of brick 74 feet in height. An inscription in the northern face of the tower shews that it was erected in the time of the Moghul Emperor Humáyun, who reigned 1530–1556 A. D. The mound is regarded as being formed by the remains of another tower of the same age as, and probably much loftier than the Dhamek. Visitors may ascend to the top of the Chaukandi, from which a good view of the surrounding country with a glimpse of the distant city and the minarets may be obtained.

TOWN HALL, THE. This is a fine building of brick pointed with Chunar stone, built in the mixed Hindu and Moorish style common to Benares. The main hall is seventy three feet long and thirty two feet wide, and will seat between three and four hundred persons. There are two fine portraits in oils in the hall, one of the donor of the Hall, the Mahárájá of Vizianagram, and the other of H. F. Tucker, Esq., who was Commissioner of Benares during the mutiny, and whose memory as a Christian gentleman is revered among natives to this day. Miss Tucker, better known as A. L. O. E., was his sister. Over the entrance to the Hall is a marble slab with the following inscription :—

ALFRED HALL.

"This Hall was built by H. H. the Maharajah of Vizianagram, K. C. S. I., to commemorate the visit of H. R. H., Prince Alfred to the city in June, 1870. It was commenced in 1873, completed in 1875, and opened by H. R. H. the Prince of Wales in 1876, when it was presented as a free gift to the citizens of Benares."

Opposite the Town Hall is the Maidagin Tank and Gardens. The latter form an agreeable promenade, much appreciated by the residents in this crowded part of the city. In the tank is a large number of fish of a kind called rohu, some of which are of a very large size and are so tame as to approach the landing place, where they are fed by natives who regard them with great veneration.

CHAPTER IV.

Hints to Travellers.

The European in Benares could go anywhere and see anything if he would observe two simple rules, *i. e.* travel barefoot, and refrain from touching. The touch of a European hand, and above all the pressure of a shoe, made as it is from the skin of a slaughtered ox, the most sacred of animals, means defilement which the most painful washings and bathings hardly suffice to remove. To refrain from touching is easy, but to go barefoot scarcely possible, hence in some cases, and those the least important, the traveller will have to be content with views of the interiors of temples as seen from open doorways. On the walls of some of the chief temples will be observed marble tablets with requests to "gentlemen not belonging to Hindu religion" to refrain from entering the temple. These tablets are of recent date, and are due to the officious conduct of a set of men who infest these places of interest, and who have in the past, in the hope of gain, introduced travellers into sacred places without possessing the least shadow of authority. These men are called *Dalâls,* anglicé *touts,* and of them let the traveller beware. In the train of one of these men he goes as a sheep to the slaughter. They may be recognised by their broken English, their evident lack of occupation, their long sufferingness under rebuke, returning like a beaten spaniel after the most scathing sarcasm, and above all by their whole-souled devotion to the interests of the stranger within their gates.

EXCURSIONS. In arranging the following excursions attention has been paid to what is really important and characteristic in Benares. Many days might be spent in visiting and inspecting all the places mentioned in this book, and after that many more would remain for which space cannot be found. The traveller, however, who follows the itinerary here laid down will, if he have only one or twc days at his disposal, be able to obtain a very distinct picture of Benares as a religious centre. The most important and characteristic sights of Benares have been arranged for the first day's excursion.

First Day, Morning. The traveller should drive straight to *Dasaswamedh Ghát.* Before taking a boat, visit the *Mánmandir Observatory*, page 67. Before embarking, the carriage should be sent to the Chauk, if the tourist decides to walk through the city streets from the Minarets, otherwise it should remain. Proceeding *up* the stream the *Ghâts* are passed one by one, page 37. On proceeding as far as is thought necessary the boat should be turned *down* stream. Arriving at the *Burning Ghát*, page 47, the traveller should alight and examine the *Manikarniká Kund*, page 50, and the *Charana Páduká*, page 50, and then re-embark at the ruined *Scindia Ghát*, page 52. Proceeding down the river as far as *Pánch Gangá Ghàt*, page 54, the traveller should disembark and climb the *Minarets*, page 61. From thence he may return to the boat, or better still, dismiss the boat and walk through the narrow streets to the Chauk, thence to the *Gyán Bápi Mosque* page 57 the *Gyán Bápi Well* page 56, the *Golden Temple*, page 55, *Sanichar's Temple*, page 75, *Anna Purna Temple*, page 29, *Sákhi Binàyak Temple*, page 75, by which time he will probably feel he has had enough for one morning.

First Day Afternoon. A visit to *Sárnáth*, page 75, is quite sufficient for the afternoon; or the following may be preferred :—

The Monkey Temple, page 64, *Lolarik Kuán*, page 61, ending with a drive through the crowded Chauk.

Second Day Morning. *Bakariya Kund*, page 31, *Lát Bhairo*, page 60, *Ráj Ghát Plateau*, page 72, *Barná Sangam*, page 32, *Ganj Shahid Mosque*, page 36, *Arhái Kangura Mosque*, page 30, *Kámeshwar Temple*, page 60 and return home past the Fruit Market, *Town Hall*, page 78, Prince of Wales and Dufferin Hospitals.

Second Day Afternoon. The *Pisách Mochan tank*, page 71, *Queen's College* and grounds, page 72, *Bará Ganesh Temple*, page 31, *Jain Temple*, page 59, *Bhaironáth Temple*, page 33, *Dandpán* and *Well of Fate*, page 35, *Briddh Kál*, page 34, *Nág Kuan*, page 67 and return via Dáránagar and part of the Ráj Ghát road, over the Iron Bridge and past the Blind Asylum and Cemeteries.

Moonlight River Excursion.

A visit to the Gháts by moonlight is a very interesting experience and if the season be favourable the visitor will do well to avail himself of the opportunity. Arrangements should be made for a boat to be ready at Assi Ghát to which place the visitor may proceed by road. On embarkation the carriage should be sent on to await the traveller at Dasaswamedh Ghát.

As the boat drops down with the current the gháts come slowly into view one by one. The moonlight, clear and cold, brings out with almost startling clearness the white temples and shrines, flinging shadows of inky blackness here and there. The steps, usually so crowded, are now deserted, save where here and there the tiny ray of some hermit's lamp is seen glimmering in some dark corner, or it may be that from some monastery or temple comes the sound of weird music or chanting telling of special vigils being kept by devoted worshippers. Occasionally religious festivals are held on the river at night, when the surface of the stream is covered with boats and barges, brilliantly decorated and illuminated with coloured lamps and filled to overflowing with brightly dressed pleasure seekers.

INDEX.

	Page.
Anna Púrná temple	29
Arhái Kangura mosque ...	30
Bakariya Kund	31
Bará Ganesh temple	31
Barná Sangam	32
Bhaironáth temple	33
Brass ware	3
Briddhkal temple	34
Buddhistic remains	35
Charana Páduká	50
Cheit Singh's Rebellion ...	14
Church, St. Mary's	74
Cow Temple, see Anna Púrná	
Dálbhyeswar temple	46
Dandpán temple	35
Dharm Kúp...	46
Dufferin Bridge	1
Durga Kund, see Monkey temple	
Excursions	79
Ganj Shahid Mosque	36
Gauri Kund, see Kidár Ghát	
Ghát, Agneswar	53
,, Ahlya Bai	40
,, Assi Sangam	45
,, Bachráj	43
,, Báji Ráo	44
,, Barna Sangam... ...	55
,, Brahmá	54
,, Burning or Jalsain ...	47
,, Chauki	41
,, Chausathi	40
,, Dandi...	43
,, Dasaswámedh	38
,, Durgá	54
,, Gái	55
Ghát, Gangá Mahal	53
,, Ghonsla	53
,, Hanumán	43
,, Jánki	44
,, Kidár	41
,, Lakshman Bálá ...	53
,, Lálá Misr	44
,, Lalita	46
,, Mádho Rái	54
,, Manikarniká	49
,, Mán mandir	45
,, Mánsarwar	41
,, Mashán	42
,, Mir	46
,, Munshi	40
,, Nárad...	41
,, Pánch Gangá	54
,, Pánde	41
,, Prahlád	55
,, Rájá	41
,, Ráj mandir	54
,, Rájrajeswari	47
,, Rám	53
,, Rána Mahal	40
,, Sankatá	52
,, Scindia	52
,, Shivála	43
,, Sitalá	55
,, Someswar	41
,, Trilochan	55
,, Tulsi	44
Golden Temple	55
Gyán Bapi Well	56
,, ,, Mosque	57
Hackney carriages, Hire of ...	84

	Page.
Jain temple	59
Kal Kup, see Dandpán	
Kámeshwar temple	60
Kádár náth temple, ...	42
Lát Bhairo	60
Lolárik Kuán	61
Manikarniká Kund	50
Minarets, The	61
Missionary Societies	62
Monkey temple	64
Nág Kuán	57
Nepaulese temple	46
Observatory, The	67
Panch Kosi Road	69
Pisách Mochan tank	71

	Page.
Queen's College	72
Ráj Ghát Plateau	72
Rám Nagar Fort	73
Sákhi Binàyak temple	75
Sanichar temple	75
Sárnáth	75
Serpents' Well	67
Small-pox temple	39
Town Hall	78
Warren Hastings in Benares ...	14
Wazir Alí's Revolt	17
Well of Fate	35
Well of Knowledge, see Gyán Bápi.	

RATES OF HIRE OF HACKNEY CARRIAGES.

1. *Fares by time within the limits of Benares Municipality and Cantonments.*

First Class.	R.	A.	P.
For first hour or fraction of an hour...	0	12	0
For every subsequent hour up to 3 hours...	0	6	0
Over 3 hours for each hour ...	0	4	0
Second Class.			
For the first hour or fraction of an hour...	0	8	0
For every subsequent hour or fraction of an hour up to 5 hours...	0	4	0
For a day of 9 hours	2	0	0

2. *Special rates between certain points.*

	1st class.			2nd class.		
From Cantonment and Civil Statíon to Ráj Ghat and vice versa ...	1	0	0	0	10	0
,, ,, to Harrowah and vice versa...	1	8	0	1	0	0
,, ,, to Sarnath and back...	2	8	0	2	0	0

N. B.—Return fares shall be charged at half the above rates provided the return journey be commenced within one hour from the time of arrival, but if the passenger oversteps the said hour, additional rates by time may be charged for the further period to the commencement of the return journey.